LYM

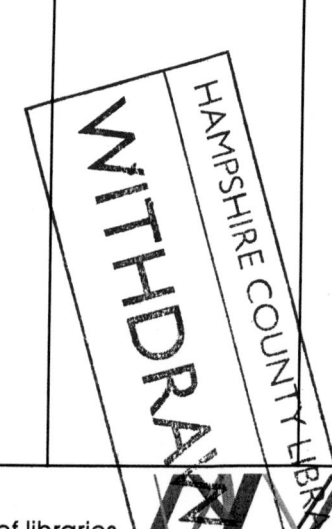

Get **more** out of libraries

Please return or renew this item by the last date shown.

You can renew online at www.hants.gov.uk/library

Or by phoning 0300 555 1387

Hampshire
County Council

D1357713

C016004143

The River Cottage

Pigs & Pork Handbook

The River Cottage Pigs & Pork Handbook

by Gill Meller

with an introduction by
Hugh Fearnley-Whittingstall

rivercottage.net

BLOOMSBURY
LONDON · NEW DELHI · NEW YORK · SYDNEY

For all the great cooks I have worked with,
learnt from and laughed with

First published in Great Britain 2015

Text © 2015 by Gill Meller,
except the preface on pp.6–7 © 2015 by Hugh Fearnley-Whittingstall.
Photography © 2015 by Gavin Kingcome,
except the following: p.15 © David Chapman/Alamy; p.35 © FLPA/Alamy; p.43 © MARCELODLT/
Shutterstock; pp.48 and 51 © Animal Photography, Sally Anne Thompson.

The publishers would like to thank the following for their help with photography locations:
Bellair Haye Pork (felicitysfarmshop.co.uk) pp.16 and 46; Magdalen Farm (magdalenfarm.org.uk) p.47;
Oakland Pigs (oaklandpigs.co.uk) cover and pp.8–9, 20, 40–41, 50 and 58 (bottom); Smallicombe Farm
(smallicombe.com) pp.2–3, 26–7, 30, 33, 44, 66 and 256.

The moral right of the author has been asserted

Bloomsbury Publishing Plc, 50 Bedford Square, London WC1B 3DP
bloomsbury.com
Bloomsbury is a trademark of Bloomsbury Publishing Plc
Bloomsbury Publishing, London, New Delhi, New York and Sydney

A CIP catalogue record for this book is available from the British Library
ISBN 978 1 4088 1792 6
10 9 8 7 6 5 4 3 2 1

Project editor: Janet Illsley
Designer: Will Webb
Photographer: Gavin Kingcome
Indexer: Hilary Bird

Printed and bound in Italy by Graphicom

While every effort has been made to ensure the accuracy of the information contained in this book, in no
circumstances can the publisher or the author accept any legal responsibility or liability for any loss or
damage (including damage to property and/or personal injury) arising from any error in or omission from
the information contained in this book, or from the failure of the reader to properly and accurately follow
any instructions contained in the book. The recipes supplied in the book are for personal use only. No recipe
may be used for commercial purposes without the express permission of the author.

bloomsbury.com/rivercottage
rivercottage.net

Contents

Gill and I first bonded over the rather battered second-hand stove that dominated the tiny kitchen of the original River Cottage HQ, near Bridport in West Dorset. Things were fairly hand-to-mouth in those days – I recall a lot of weather and a lot of mud, and not infrequent power cuts and fridge failures (a motivating factor, perhaps, in the rapid development of our meat-curing skills).

But I also remember a huge amount of fun and some really spectacular feasts, all based, of course, on fantastic seasonal produce from the land around us. The learning curve was steep, but it led us inexorably to the River Cottage organic smallholding and cookery school that thrives today at Park Farm, near Axminster, where Gill is now our Group Head Chef. And I'd be lost without him.

Gill has cooked beside me, for me, and sometimes in competition with me, countless times over the last decade. His creativity, curiosity and sheer verve have infiltrated my own cooking and my thinking about food so that I barely know where his kitchen ends and mine begins. Coupled with that originality is a rock-solid ability and true mastery of his craft. He's a good butcher and a fine baker, as well as a great chef. He knows how to hone smart ideas into dependable recipes you can cook at home. In short, he's as good a friend as you could hope for in a kitchen.

But this book, of course, goes beyond the kitchen. And this reflects another of Gill's qualities, namely that he's just as likely to be seen in a pair of muddy wellies as in his chef's whites. The garden, farm and field are as important to him as the kitchen – not because he doesn't love to cook above all else, but precisely because he does. Everyone who works at River Cottage understands the significance of the origin of ingredients and that you can't really be a good cook if you don't know what you're cooking with. But Gill has a commitment to sustainable, ethical sourcing and a passion for provenance that's second to none, myself included.

When it comes to pigs, we know that sourcing and provenance could not be more important – the quality of the animal's life defines the quality of its meat – and Gill is the ideal person to demonstrate the River Cottage ethos and enthusiasm for these wonderful animals and their fantastic meat. Gill walks our porky talk.

Pigs have always been at the heart of River Cottage. I bought a pair of Gloucester Old Spots when I first moved to Dorset, and I've kept pigs ever since. At River Cottage HQ, we now raise up to twenty each year – Old Spots, Saddlebacks and Oxford Sandy and Blacks are our favourite breeds. Our Pig in a Day courses, where guests learn how to butcher a whole pig and then cook amazing things with the various cuts, were among the first we launched and remain incredibly popular.

This is partly because a lot of people really love pork. And of course, many of us like pigs too; they are appealing, gregarious, intelligent animals, easy to look after and very handy when it comes to recycling garden scraps. But I think more and more people are also recognising something a little less savoury about pigs: they are the best (or rather, sadly, the worst) example of what has gone wrong in our relationship with meat. And the growing enthusiasm for small-scale outdoor pig rearing is an encouraging vote for how it could be put right.

Less than a century ago, pigs were domestic livestock in the true sense – kept by small-scale farmers and some of the poorest households – respected and well-cared-for in anticipation of the meaty cuts, offal and charcuterie they would yield. Now, however, pigs have become the unfortunate standard-bearers for all that is shameful in our meat industry. Abused, manipulated, confined and medicated, factory-farmed pigs are among the most wretched creatures on the planet. And the meat we derive from them – all that cheap bacon and bland sausage – is miserable too.

But pig lovers all over the land are demonstrating that we can reject this modern model of inhumane farming and release ourselves from the clutches of the industrial food giants. You may want to make the full commitment of keeping pigs, but even if you don't, you need only be a savvy shopper and a thrifty cook to find, prepare and enjoy great pork the way it should be enjoyed, with a clear conscience. This book tells you all you need to know to set out on either of those paths.

It's been a fiercely held tenet of mine for many years that the closer we can get to the source of our food, and the more involved we can be in its preparation, the better. Being informed about what you buy and in control of what you feed to your family and friends is empowering and leads to a richer, healthier, more fulfilling daily life. Books like this one, and experts like Gill, are crucial in the quest for that greater understanding. Whether you want to go the whole hog (as it were) and buy your own pigs, or you simply want to eat better bacon (and you will not eat better, I promise you, than bacon you've cured yourself), Gill's knowledgeable, detailed and often drily witty words open the door.

I love Gill's recipes, many of which I know intimately, as they have been honed over the decade of our partnership. The wonderful balance he strikes between irresistible, comforting classics (roast pork belly and crackling; rillettes; sausage rolls) and eye-opening new ideas (pig's tail with damsons; crispy pig's ears with mayo) is enough to keep any cook happy. And his detailed step-by-step instructions on basic pork butchery will have you sharpening your knives before you know it.

But what I appreciate most about this book is its holistic approach. Gill's passion for, and knowledge of, great pork cookery radiate from the page, but so does his fascination and respect for the pig as a sensitive, sociable creature – from the wild boar of old to the varied breeds of today. He is determined that welfare and good husbandry should be held in as high esteem as flavour and texture. And, of course, he eloquently espouses the vital connection between these things. If everyone regarded the venerable pig in this way, it's not just the animals that would be better off: all of us who cook and eat meat would be part of a richer and finer culture.

Hugh Fearnley-Whittingstall, East Devon, December 2014

About Pigs

We are a nation of pork lovers, but I would like us to be a nation of pig lovers, too.

Pigs and pork play a big part in my life. I have the good fortune to work at Park Farm, a smallholding producing its own pork in a simple and respectful way, following the organic model. I see how the pigs are raised and cared for. I know how they live, what they eat and how they die. This gives me a sense of pride, because I know these pigs have been treated well. But beyond that, as a chef, it gives me great practical and professional satisfaction. I've seen first-hand how welfare and feeding affect the quality of the meat, and I've had the pleasure of learning how to make the absolute most of this magnificent beast.

For many chefs, the journey with pork begins with a thud. That thud is the sound of a box of cheap vac-packed bacon being delivered, just before breakfast service. It happens in hotels across the country. And through the chaos of grilled tomatoes and scrambled eggs, the vac-packs are torn open and the uniform rashers within are fried in their own watery juices before being set to wither beneath the heated gantry of the self-service breakfast bar.

To me, this kind of breakfast is no breakfast at all. More likely than not, the bacon being cooked will have come from pigs that have led an awful life, but the chefs in this scenario are not so much the villains as the victims. They are employed in a business in which the onus is generally on price and profit, at the expense of provenance and taste. Having the time to connect with the ingredients they are cooking, let alone select better ones, is almost impossible for them. Unfortunately, we, the consumers, must take some responsibility for this.

The problem is that not everyone cares about the origins of the bangers that go with their mash. Our desire for, and acceptance of, cheap pork has created a regime of supply and demand – or demand and supply, as it should be phrased – that has all but crushed ethical, free-range pig farming. The industry has capitalised on this animal's capacity to adapt to less than ideal conditions and rolled out intensive farming on a monstrous scale, throwing up appalling welfare issues. At least half of the 10 million pigs we kill each year in Britain will never have seen the sky or felt grass under their feet. Sadly, we have managed to disassociate ourselves from the actual origin of the pork we eat.

Some people might think that watching a tribe of mischievous piglets going about their day hasn't the faintest thing to do with good food or cooking, but they'd be wrong. It has everything to do with it. Seeing the food we love to eat in the context of its natural environment – be it vegetables and salads growing in the garden or a few pigs in the paddock – is a crucial element in understanding it and thereby making considered decisions about what we should really be eating.

Being involved in the lives of the pigs at River Cottage has given me a profound respect for these intelligent and inquisitive creatures and the tradition and history

A prosciutto ham air-drying in the garden shed

of farming them. Through preparing and cooking the pork they provide, I've learnt a lot about the economics of food and about thrift. But perhaps most importantly, I've seen the value of understanding an ingredient and its provenance: knowledge that is the foundation of any good recipe.

My well-worn and broken-spined copy of Jane Grigson's *Charcuterie and French Pork Cookery*, first published in 1969, enshrines a nose-to-tail approach to pork cookery that we have largely lost. It is, however, an approach I try to adopt across the board. Whether I'm preparing a rabbit or a radish, the principle is the same: waste nothing. This philosophy has a particular resonance when used in the context of the pig, partly because it's a living creature and using it all up demonstrates a basic respect for it, but also because it is uniquely versatile in the kitchen. No other animal gives us such a range of different end products, from lard to liver, cheeks to chops, pâté to prosciutto. We really ought to be using everything but the oink – and that should and can be a pleasure, not a burden.

Perhaps it's because of this versatility that pigs have become wholly entwined in the food culture of so many civilisations, dating back thousands of years. This book begins by exploring that chequered history and looks at how the successful domestication of pigs has made pork the most consumed meat in the world.

If you're interested in joining the age-old tradition of pig keeping, you'll find what you need to know in this book. Raising your own pigs is a commitment but it's a truly rewarding one from which everyone and everything involved will benefit. You don't have to be rich and you don't need acres of land to do it. I've put together a 'pig keeper's rough guide' that I hope will give you the confidence to have a go yourself. As an adjunct to this section – and also useful if you're able to buy in whole or half carcasses from a local producer – I've provided all the instructions you'll need to butcher a pig at home, producing all our most familiar cuts and a few you may have yet to try.

If you're not ready to take the plunge and buy your own weaners just yet, you can satisfy your quest for well-raised local pork by simply buying the right stuff from the right place. I'll show you what to look out for: with a good sourcing strategy in place, you'll be supporting conscientious farmers, the rural economy and the on-going fight for real, slow-grown food.

I have also included recipes for some proper classics, from simple roast pork belly (p.196) to pâté de campagne (p.208) as well as less familiar recipes such as traditional faggots (p.140) and pressed pig's cheek terrine (p.225). It is, after all, dishes like these that have made the pig what it is today.

I hope that I can show you that by taking a holistic approach – considering not just the meat on your plate but the noble creature that provided it and the processes that have brought it to you – you will derive even more enjoyment from this wonderful ingredient.

A potted history of pigs

Since I was a boy, I've been fascinated by birds of prey. Their intelligence has always captivated me, and so has the history of these fine-tuned predators as hunting companions to man. I've been flying hawks and falcons myself for many years; it's something I love to do, and it led me to an experience I will never forget.

I was hunting one of my hawks through scrubland on the edge of Powerstock Common in Dorset. The terrain was rough, with an eerie remoteness. I came into a large clearing of grasses, sporadic bramble and soft marsh. My hawk swooped past me and alighted on a small spinney of young willow and bramble. I assumed the barely discernible movement of a rabbit or pheasant in the undergrowth had caught his eye. I went right up to the tangle of blackberry with the intention of flushing out whatever was inside.

All of a sudden, the entire bush erupted in the most dramatic way. The ground literally shook as, from within, out barged the barrelling frame of the biggest wild boar I'd ever seen. The shock of its physical stature took me from my feet and, as I fell, it hoofed over my left leg and down through the copse. I quickly gathered my thoughts before bolting in the opposite direction. It was quite a meeting. On this occasion, I'm sure the boar was as alarmed as I was. Had she been with piglets, however, things could have turned out rather less well for me. I would have stood no chance against this powerful wild animal if she was, quite legitimately, protecting her young.

Powerstock Common is made up of several thousand acres of wild woodland interspersed with ancient grazing pasture. It represents a type of landscape, now largely lost, that would once have been widespread in the British Isles. Wild boar live there today in the same way they have done for many centuries, with little or no intervention from man. They are free to prowl the forest in the evergreen half-light, largely unnoticed, though areas of broken, turned ground are evidence that these powerful foragers are not far away.

Truly 'wild' wild boar are rare in Britain today but that wasn't always the case. Large family groups or 'sounders' were prolific throughout ancient Britain. They were omnivorous scavengers just like our modern-day pigs, though they preferred to forage under cover of darkness. Due to their mixed natural diet and muscle build their meat was lean and full of flavour – an invaluable source of protein for early hunter-gatherers who would have tracked and killed them. Their meat would have been cooked over open fires, their bones utilised for tools and weapons, their thick skin tanned for leather clothes, and even their bristles used for making brushes.

These early primitive pigs (*Sus scrofa*) could be found all over the globe, ranging across mixed climates and habitats. They were first domesticated somewhere in the Near East around 9,000 years ago and, independently, a little later in Europe. This was a transitional time when Neolithic hunters were becoming farmers, not long after the first plants became domesticated. The pig, being such an adaptable omnivore, thrived in this new environment and soon became invaluable to the daily workings of many a homestead throughout the British Isles.

For the peasant farmer, keeping a few pigs meant being able to provide meat for his family throughout the year. In addition, his pigs and piglets could provide him with wares to barter and the means to generate an income. Keeping pigs enriched the biodiversity on a farm and they often proved to be extremely useful labour-saving creatures. They would happily clear fallow or scrubland by grazing, simultaneously turning over and fertilising the ground and thereby readying it for crops and vegetables.

The pigs' unfussy disposition and less than discerning attitude towards what they ate must have rung like a happy tune for the farmers and families who kept them. Their exceptional appetite for anything remotely edible was a linchpin in their success, and their transition from forest dweller to farmyard resident proved one of evolution's less complex undertakings.

The fifteenth-century poet Gervase Markham wrote, splendidly, that the pig 'is the Husbandman's best Scavenger, and the Huswives most wholsome sink; for his food and living is by that which will else rot in the yard… for from the Husbandman he taketh pulse, chaff, barn dust, man's ordure, garbage, and the weeds of his yard;

Wild boar

British Lops enjoying some fresh pasture

and from the huswife her draff, swillings, whey, washing of tubs, and such like – with which he will live and keep a good state of body, very sufficiently'.

Over centuries, pigs adapted to the areas and climates they lived in, resulting in the wonderful regional diversity we see today. Some very old breeds have long since died out, but some, with stronger bloodlines, still endure. Their colouring, shape and size have all been influenced by their local environments – as, of course, has the taste of the meat they provide.

As villages grew into towns and those towns into cities, pigs happily followed man into the urban sprawl. It seemed there was always a place for the pig. In the 1300s London was full of piggeries and they were swelling beyond control. Their keepers would routinely let pigs out into the streets to scavenge and fatten up and, although city pigs dealt with decomposing waste, they produced a lot too, and they soon became a health hazard themselves. There are stories of whole families of pigs living in the sewers of Hampstead and in 1850 Shepherd's Bush was dubbed 'the pigsty of the metropolis' because nearly every house kept some of the animals. At about the same time health inspectors discovered 3,000 pigs in the Potteries (now Notting Hill), distributed between 250 squalid properties.

Pigs also found their way into industry. They were kept in large numbers by dairies, distilleries and starch-makers who fattened them up on waste grain and buttermilk for slaughter, a conversion that made perfect financial sense, providing these businesses with a lucrative sideline income.

For families throughout Europe, the annual pig slaughter assumed traditional importance. They would carry out their own time-honoured slaughter practices, and go on to use recipes passed down from generation to generation. Generally the family pig, having reaped the green pastures of spring and the gluts of high summer, would be killed in the autumn in prime condition. The processing of the animal usually took place out of doors, and the meat could be stored during the cooler months of late autumn and early winter without spoiling. The meat, both fresh and cured, provided sustenance and protein throughout the lean and bitter months, bringing abundance and generosity over the Christmas period in particular.

Even today, the slaughter of a pig continues to be a significant event for families who keep a hog at home. The killing itself may now take place in an abattoir but the processing of the meat into a range of delicious products can still take a very similar form. One of the beauties of this tradition is the way the foods created out of necessity have now become classic ingredients. In a time before refrigeration, the arts of salting, smoking and drying were essential in order to preserve the bulk of the meat yielded by a pig, and so products such as bacon, salami and chorizo were developed. We no longer strictly need to cure pork in this way but we have come to love these ingredients, the art of making them still thrives, and they continue to underpin many of the world's great cuisines to this day.

Pig farming today

British agriculture is changing. Due to the demands of our growing population farming is unrecognisable from the way it was 50 years ago. Take British cherry production as an example. Business is booming, demand is up, so year on year we are growing more cherries, in less space, more quickly and more cheaply.

Clever rootstock grafting has taken the best the cherry-red gene pool has to offer, breeding trees with characteristics such as low-growing, easy-to-pick fruit, suited to industrial-scale production. This means that there are now very few productive traditional cherry orchards around Britain. These small pockets of our rural heritage offer less consistent, less plentiful, more slowly grown fruit that has been superseded by its modern offspring in all ways bar one – and that's flavour.

Just like the traditional cherry trees, our heritage and rare pig breeds don't tick all the boxes when it comes to consistency, shape, size and colour. These animals do not adapt well to being intensively farmed and so we've carefully selected, bred and crossbred pigs that do conform. These pigs – a combination of Large White, Landrace and Welsh crosses – produce fast-growing, low-fat carcasses.

It's certainly a shame to lose our wonderful old cherry orchards, but this form of intensified food production is tolerable, even acceptable, in comparison to the horrendous issues we face when the same approach is taken with pork production. We kill around 10 million pigs a year in Britain, 70% of which have been intensively farmed. That's bad enough, but only 30% of the pork we eat in this country actually comes from British pigs. The rest is imported – from countries where welfare standards, in many cases, are so low they would be illegal in Britain.

Despite the fact that we have some of the highest welfare standards in Europe, conditions for our pigs within intensive systems are harrowing.

Imagine, if you can, that you are a breeding sow within this system. You spend the best part of your life confined, on concrete, pregnant and unable to move naturally. You are artificially inseminated at 7 months old and, after 16 weeks, produce 10–12 piglets in a farrowing crate – a cage so restrictive that you cannot stand or even roll over. You are separated from your baby piglets by bars, unable to reach them or tend to them in the way a mother naturally would.

Normally piglets are weaned at 7–10 weeks. Your piglets, however, are forcibly weaned and taken from you after 27 days, long before their immune systems have developed. One or two will die before this point anyway. You are pregnant again within a couple of weeks. You may have as many as seven litters before being slaughtered, exhausted from the endless pregnancies. You are then processed into budget sausages. You survived on a cocktail of antibiotics, administered to prevent you dying before you'd fulfilled your projected profitability, but drugs didn't help alleviate the severe discomfort and psychological stress you suffered in your life.

For your piglets things aren't any better. They may have their teeth clipped and tails docked without any form of anaesthetic, only to be consigned to overcrowded, badly lit pens or cages. The only way to deal with the volumes of faeces and urine they produce is to fit slatted floors, which means no straw – the most basic form of environmental enrichment a pig requires. A short but torturous life of frustration, antibiotics and aggression ensues. If they survive this, they face the unforgivably cramped and stressful process of being transported to slaughter where, finally, their miserable lives will end – all too regularly, in a partially stunned and brutally painful way.

Pigs pay a very high price for the very low-cost pork we consume, but the controversy surrounding intensive pig farming goes beyond poor welfare and cruelty. It's actually costing us more than we might think. We are paying for it through the loss of small independent farms and the collapse of rural economies. We're paying for it through deforestation in order to grow animal feed crops on greater scales. But, most worryingly, intensive pig farming has been shown to be affecting our own health – and that's a high price indeed. Studies show the endemic use of antibiotics to fight disease and promote growth in pigs produces drug-resistant bacteria and hyper-viral pathogens. These pass from the pig farms directly to us via pollution of the water course, the spreading of slurry on fields and the crops we eat and even through the air we breathe.

It's a very tricky situation to be in. Meeting the food demands of our booming populations is a real challenge, and some forms of intensification in farming are inevitable. But it's unacceptable for us to keep pigs in this way and things can be different. Unlike the pigs, we have a choice. We can make informed decisions about the pork we buy. Apart from enforced, government-driven legislation, we are the only arbiters of change. Orchestrating a cultural shift is a big task and one that must start at home. Reaching for high-welfare pork sausages instead of the cheapest alternative will send ripples through the pond of pork production that cannot be ignored. The more retailers source better pork, the more farmers will improve their farming methods, and the more pigs will live happier lives.

The organic alternative

The simplest way to ensure you are not encouraging the intensive pig-farming industry is to choose organic pork. Organic pigs are kept in conditions that allow them to express their natural behaviour. They are kept in family groups with unrestricted access to their fields and paddocks. In severe weather, they can come inside, provided their barns are well bedded with fresh straw and they have continued access to outdoor space. This means that most organic pigs will be outdoors for the best part of the year.

The Soil Association, Britain's most recognised certification body, is one of the original campaigning organisations for healthy, humane and sustainable food, farming and land use. The organisation forbids many of the unethical practices that are still prolific within intensive systems.

Nose ringing – the deeply uncomfortable practice of crunching a solid metal ring through the pig's highly sensitive snout in order to stop the pig from indulging in natural rooting behaviour – is banned within organic farming. Tail docking is also prohibited. Intensively farmed pigs bite each other's tails out of boredom and frustration and cutting them off when they are a few days old can stop this. However, in organic and most free-range set-ups, this is not necessary.

Farrowing crates are banned within organic farming. They are rightly considered cruel and unnecessary and there's some evidence to show that even within intensive systems they can be avoided. Because organic pigs are not crammed together in small spaces, they rarely require antibiotics. If they do, the dosing is monitored and longer withdrawal periods before the animal can be slaughtered are enforced.

Buying organic pork means you are supporting high-welfare farms, as well as a community who are working for a better future for agriculture and wildlife in general. You can nearly always guarantee the pigs have led the best possible life and that, more often than not, the farmer has reared interesting traditional breeds.

Buying pork

I don't buy vast quantities of pork, although given the subject of this book, you'd be forgiven for thinking I do. I prefer to spend a bit more on the really good stuff and not eat it quite so regularly. If I'm lucky, I get to take home the odd organic joint from River Cottage or some freshly made sausages perhaps (purely for recipe testing purposes, of course). This is good pork that has come from our pigs on the farm and is always delicious. I make the occasional piece of bacon, which is great for breakfast, and about once a year I buy a half carcass of pork, which I butcher myself. The last batch came from my good friend Robin Rea, who rears Oxford Sandy and Blacks and has his own small restaurant, the Rusty Pig, in nearby Ottery St Mary, serving the finest pork.

When looking for the best pork, whether that's joints or small products, like sausages, pâtés and pies, I'd advise anyone to go to a smaller independent retailer. They are far more likely to support local producers and farmers and will be able to talk to you about the food they sell. They may not necessarily be organic, as organic certification comes at a price. There is a significant cost to the farmer by way of an annual registration fee and carrying the organic symbol on their pork requires greater levels of documentation, auditing and transparency. For some farmers it's viable, while for others it is not.

It's worth remembering this when you're out shopping, as there are many fantastic free-range pig farmers who have the welfare of their pigs at the very top of their priorities – farmers who refuse to compromise and who produce pork that is second to none, but who have simply chosen not to meet the expense of full accreditation. This is just one reason why actually talking to the person who supplies your pork is such a good idea. You may even be able to visit the farm to see conditions for yourself.

The first place to look for good pork is a proper butcher's shop – one with sound ethics, supporting local high-welfare farms. Strike up a relationship with them, particularly if they claim to be purveyors of rare-breed and free-range fresh pork. It's perfectly reasonable for you to ask questions about what you're buying – after all, it's you and your family who are eating it. Make it clear what you're looking for. See if you can find out a bit more about the pork your butcher is selling, where it's from and the breed of pig in question.

Ask to have a look, if the meat is not out on display. Has it got a good, vigorous colour, or is it pallid and anaemic? Does it look firm and well set, or is it flaccid and moist? Has it got a nice covering of clean white fat, or is it so lean the pig could have starved to death? Is the skin dry to the touch or has it been sitting in a vac-pack, macerating in its own bloody juices? If a butcher is unhelpful or cannot name the farm where the pork has been reared, I would be sceptical about them.

Your enquiries should be well received in most butchers' shops because the retail of slow-grown local pork is an area where supermarkets cannot compete. Many of those suppliers may just be too small for the big boys to bother with.

Another great place to get good pork is a real farm shop. One near me rears its own pigs in a paddock just off the main car park. All the kids go and say hello to the pigs and give them a scratch before they go in and pick up their sausages for tea. I also know a local farm that keeps Gloucester Old Spots and sells a fantastic array of fresh and frozen cuts, including the trotters, cheeks and farm-made salami.

Farmers' markets allow you to go straight to the source when buying fresh pork, bacon and ham. Not only do you meet the farmer in person, you can discuss their wares, and hopefully witness their passion for pigs and farming. The great upside to shopping in markets like this is that the farmer gets the best possible price for their pork, which for him can make the difference between sinking and swimming. It also means that the money you spend goes back into the local rural economy, supporting the growth and development of the smaller farms that try so hard to compete with the bigger retailers.

Pork in supermarkets

Although I'd always prefer to buy my meat from a small independent producer, I'm not blind to the reality that the majority of the meat we consume in this country is sold through supermarkets. You can still make good choices in these big retailers. There are various bodies in Britain that regulate, inspect and approve baseline and higher-welfare pig farms. They can help us identify better products easily on the supermarket shelf.

For me, organic pork would always be the first choice in a supermarket because, in the absence of any other information about the source of that meat, it offers a guarantee of high welfare. Organic pork is now very widely available, although supermarket organic pork may not be British. The 'Organic' symbol is the strictest form of welfare accreditation and there are several approved organic control bodies, all of which meet EU standards. DEFRA (Department for Environment, Food and Rural Affairs) is responsible for organic farming standards in Britain.

If you cannot, or don't want to, buy organic, choose products that carry the 'Freedom Food' logo over similar products that don't. Freedom Food is a farm assurance scheme monitored by the RSPCA and any farms associated with this scheme have to meet certain welfare standards. However, the Freedom Food sticker doesn't necessarily mean the pork chops you're about to grill have come from a pig that has led a completely natural outdoor life. Compliance is staggered across levels of intensity from deep-bedded barn-reared pigs through to outdoor-bred and outdoor-reared. The label should state clearly how the pigs used in that product have lived, but unfortunately for the consumer there is still confusion.

The Soil Association certification symbol

This is because, unlike in egg and chicken production, there is no legal definition of the terms 'free-range' or 'barn-reared' for pigs. What these terms actually mean is hard to interpret.

The National Farmers' Union (NFU) launched another food assurance scheme, The Red Tractor, in 2000. It runs on a not-for-profit basis with its administrative costs being met by membership fees and licence payments. The Red Tractor logo guarantees that certain welfare expectations have been met, standards dictated by a board of representatives from across the sector. You'll find this logo on packaged fresh pork and processed foods and ready meals containing pork as its major ingredient. You'll also come across it on a whole range of other products from soft fruits to dairy products.

By choosing Red Tractor, you'll be supporting UK farmers who are conscientious enough to want to be part of an accreditation programme. However, the exact nature of any one farmer's practice can be difficult to ascertain because, although they are inspected, there is on-going confusion between baseline and higher-level welfare within the scheme. You can't be 100% sure of good animal welfare just by looking at the label.

The Food Standards Agency (FSA) maintains close contact with all assurance schemes, independently monitoring their consumer communications and claims, and checking their accuracy, reassuringly enforcing good practice.

Getting Started

I've always felt that doing something yourself is more rewarding than getting someone else to do it for you and when it comes to food, the results will, almost always, be considerably more delicious than any shop-bought alternative. Whether you're baking a cake or a simple loaf of bread, a fish pie or sausage rolls, you'll spend time selecting and gathering your ingredients. You'll think about the recipe and consider the process. You'll apply yourself in a practical fashion, and as a result of all that hard work, you'll produce something that tastes great.

The same goes for producing pork. You don't have to keep your own pigs in order to enjoy really good, high-welfare meat. There are lots of small-scale organic and free-range pig keepers producing excellent pork with care and compassion. However, if you want to guarantee you are eating the very best pork, from pigs that you know for certain have led a happy and contented outdoor life, there is nothing to compare with raising them yourself.

Imagine you've spent 9 months looking after your own little pigs. You've made them a home, fed and watered them, tended to their every need. They've grown big, been humanely dispatched and now it's time to roast the first joint for your Sunday lunch – could it get any better? No. Could it taste any better? I doubt it.

Keeping a couple of pigs at home is the antithesis of the industrial-scale factory farming that now dominates pork production. And just two or three pigs are all you need to reap the benefits. Such small-scale pig rearing is sustainable, ethical and the ultimate way to source the best pork for your family and friends.

In a blind tasting, I believe I could easily differentiate between free-range and factory-farmed pork. But, if you served me two different traditional breeds, both reared on the same farm, at the same time, on the same diet, by the same caring keeper, could my discerning palate pick out the unique notes of the Tamworth against the robust savour of the much-loved Saddleback? The truth is, I think not.

I don't see this as a gastronomic failing, it simply illustrates that the major factor influencing the flavour of pork is the life the pig has led. I've cooked and eaten more than my fair share of pork over the years, from a variety of different breeds, and I am in no doubt that if you are raising your own pork – and get it right, which is not hard – you'll be richly rewarded with the most delicious pork you've ever eaten.

The age of the animal is also crucial. A young animal will be quite different from an older one, in both taste and texture. At River Cottage, our older pigs (8 months and over) seem to taste better and fuller. The meat seems to 'set' better (see p.78) and the texture is more interesting. There's a distinct difference in the structure and grain of the meat: its fat appears firmer, and the muscle is darker in colour.

I attribute this superior quality to the extra life the pigs have been afforded, that extra season they've enjoyed and the greater variety of fruits and fodder offered to them during their extended period of grace. The fat they've put down and the muscle they've built up also improve flavour.

Keeping pigs

There are two main approaches to pig keeping: you either keep a sow and breed your own piglets, or buy a few weaners from a reputable pig breeder or farmer and fatten them up at home until they are ready for slaughter. If you are new to pig keeping, I'd suggest the latter option. It's more straightforward and will allow you to gain the knowledge and experience you'll need to go on and actually breed your own pigs in the future.

Buying weaners

Weaners tend to be available at between 8 and 12 weeks old. At this stage they will have stopped feeding on their mother's milk and will be on a diet of solid foods; i.e. they will be 'weaned'. It's best to get several piglets from the same litter as they will most likely all get along already and settle more comfortably in their new home. You can, of course, rear mixed litters and even breeds, but it's worth making sure they are all of a similar size and age.

Choose healthy, bright-eyed piglets who look lively, with a spring in their step. If you notice any traces of diarrhoea on the piglets or in their pen or paddock, it might be an indication that they have scour, a disease of the gut (see p.68); these animals should be avoided.

Before setting off to buy your piglets, you'll need to think about how you get them home. If you have a trailer for your vehicle then you can use an area of this, partitioned off with some sturdy plywood or boarding. It must be disinfected and clean. If you do not own or have access to a trailer, a large puppy crate, well lined with straw, will do the job – just make sure that it fits in your car. Little pigs can be noisy when you pick them up – very noisy. You must be calm, collected and confident. Get them into your chosen mode of transport with minimal fuss and they should settle down quite quickly.

Once your piglets are home, get them into their new ark. Give them time to settle and, if it's late in the day, leave them in the ark overnight before letting them out into the paddock.

At River Cottage, we keep a mixture of boars (males) and gilts (females yet to have their first litter). We keep both sexes together in the same paddock and they seem to get on pretty well. However, it is important to send boars to slaughter before they reach sexual maturity, at about 8 or 9 months old. Otherwise, they will try and mate with the gilts, which is not at all desirable if they are from the same litter. If you plan to grow your boars on for a little longer, they should be separated from the gilts by a fence.

As a general rule, our piglets arrive in spring and are slaughtered before the winter. Our paddocks sit at the base of a broad, steep hill of gorse and bracken,

Young Berkshire pigs

and, as a result, can get quite wet in bad weather. Pigs don't like living in cold, wet, muddy conditions and because we don't have the facilities to bring them in when the weather's bad, we don't overwinter pigs at River Cottage. Instead, they spend the best part of their lives enjoying good weather and plenty of fresh fruit and vegetables from the garden.

A weaner will cost somewhere between £30 and £70, depending on the farmer, the breed of pig and its bloodline. But that's not the only cost involved. You will have to buy feed, which can work out as much as £100 per piglet in total. You will also have the one-off cost of setting up your pigs' home. This will include fencing an area of ground to create a paddock and investing in an ark to provide essential shelter (see pp.54–9), as well as installing drinking and feeding facilities within the paddock itself (see p.64). And you have slaughter costs on top of all that.

Breeding pigs

It is very rewarding to breed pigs, in more ways than one. It's fantastic to play a part in this natural cycle, but it is also self-sustaining. You should be able to generate enough income from a small-scale breeding programme to cover a substantial proportion of your pig-related outgoings, as well as providing yourself with superb home-grown meat.

Pig breeding follows a year-round cycle and is somewhat more involved than simply rearing pigs for meat. There are some key decisions that will need to be made early on, the first being the scale of your breeding programme. If you intend to breed your own pigs, you'll need a breeding gilt or sow (a female who has already had a litter) and a boar to 'serve' her. Owning a boar will require an extra investment of both money and time so, unless you have big pig-production plans, it may not be worth the added expense. If you envisage a small-scale affair, you don't need to own a boar yourself; you can borrow or hire a suitable candidate instead.

A healthy gilt or sow can have two litters a year, and each litter can include 10–12 little piglets. So, if one gilt or sow can produce 20–25 piglets a year, you'll appreciate how keeping just three or four breeding stock makes you a fully fledged pig farmer. Hiring, rather than owning, a boar means you can keep everything at a manageable level.

It may be that you just want one gilt 'in pig', and only once a year. You can either bring the majority of these piglets on to slaughter weight yourself, or you can sell them as weaners and generate an income from your efforts that way. Rearing all the piglets yourself will give you plenty of fresh pork to sell and more than enough to keep you and your family well fed for the coming year.

The breeding stock you use must be right. An unimpressive sow with a bad attitude and lack of character may not produce outstanding piglets. Look for a pig with a gentle temperament, strong legs and good conformation, and make sure she is a pig you like, and that she likes you. She may be with you for several years. The same is true of a boar: it's worth shopping around for a high-quality specimen.

Gilts will first come into season at 6 or 7 months old but will not reach proper sexual maturity for a further 4 or 5 months and should not be bred from until then, to allow time for their sexual organs to develop properly. A young boar will be ready to serve gilts from 7 or 8 months.

Gilts have a 21-day cycle and will be in estrus, or 'on heat', for just a few days over this period. They should be mated, 'served' or 'serviced' by the boar at that time, so you must think about the timings carefully and look out for the signs. The most common behavioural sign of estrus is the gilt standing as if ready to be mounted by the boar. She may well stay rigid, even when her keeper applies pressure to her back. There will be some swelling or reddening to the vulva, and she may appear restless with a lack of appetite.

The gestation period

With pigs, the gestation period is 113 days, or put another way, 3 months, 3 weeks and 3 days. If you have a litter born by January and a second by June, it will mean that during the coldest parts of the year your young pigs are either with their mother suckling or fully grown and able to look after themselves.

'Farrowing' is the term used to describe the point at which the expectant mother gives birth. It can be a stressful time for both pig and keeper, and some planning is required to give your new arrivals the best chance of survival. Newborn piglets are fragile creatures. They enter the world without the capacity to fight disease.

Preparing for the piglets' arrival

Two weeks before the end of the pregnancy, the mother should be treated for internal and external parasites, as well as being vaccinated against erysipelas (see p.68). If she is treated at the correct time the benefits will be passed on to her litter. It's also about this time that your gilt or sow should be separated from other pigs that you may be keeping. This will give her time and space to settle before farrowing. Tussling and barging for food with her peers may cause undue stress and possibly pain at such an important time.

You will need a farrowing ark or some other suitable space during this last period of pregnancy. A well-bedded stable is ideal, although you can buy purpose-made farrowing arks. Alternatively, you can modify a large standard ark. Farrowing arks are designed to make the birth comfortable, practical and safe for both mother and piglets. Newborn piglets are so small that it's not uncommon for them to be accidentally crushed by their mother when she lies down to rest. This is one of the reasons why farrowing crates are used in intensive pig production, but these controversial contraptions are quite unnecessary. In fact, it's now proven that

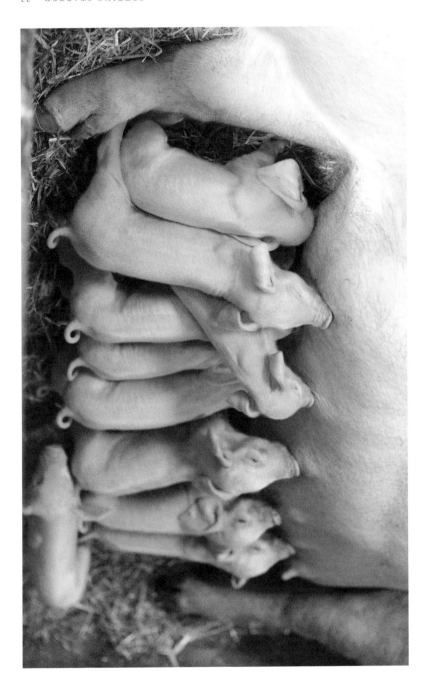

mortality rates are far lower than once thought in well-managed, deep-bedded, open farrowing barns. And if you are breeding on a very small scale, such accidents should be avoidable.

Arks should be sited on level ground and, if possible, have some form of insulation to keep them cool in the summer and warm in the winter. Ventilation is essential to help keep the air flowing and clean.

Usually a 'creep area' is integrated into farrowing arks, enabling the piglets to move safely out of their mother's way should they need to. This space, often a partitioned area adjoining the ark, is inaccessible to the mother and also provides the piglets with an area to eat solid feed later on. Once your pig has farrowed, and provided her mothering instincts are good, she should be incredibly considerate and careful not to lie on her new piglets. In fact, she will sniff and shift the straw around to see if any of her piglets are there before lying down.

Large outdoor pigs are hardy creatures but their newborn piglets won't be: cold can kill them very quickly. In very cold weather, some stockmen use heat lamps to keep the young pigs warm, though more often than not, 'mum' will take care of this job by creating a nest within her ark and tending to her young in her natural way. Make sure your pigs don't farrow while you're on holiday or otherwise engaged, as you'll need to be present to help out should it be necessary.

Birth and the first few weeks

On the day your pig gives birth, her abdomen will be very low set, almost touching the ground. She will appear restless and may hoof around her pen in an anxious state. She will move straw and generally prepare herself and her nest for the ensuing labour. It's worth bearing in mind that this is a stressful time for the mother-to-be. You will need to be as calm as possible when you are around her. She may not want you bothering or fussing, and will probably let you know it if you get in her way.

Before the piglets are born, she will lie down, her breathing will be heavy and her vulva noticeably swollen. Have some warm water on hand and wear some old clothes, as birthing can be a messy affair. The piglets will arrive one by one, often unassisted and head first. However, now and then you may need to intervene. The piglets can occasionally come out in their own sack – this may be torn but still present. If this is the case it will need to be carefully removed and the piglet wiped down with a clean towel. Make sure that the nose and mouth are clear and the piglet is breathing. You shouldn't need to cut or tie the umbilical cord as this tends to break as the piglet presents.

If you have the space, the newly born piglets can be kept in a creep area until the birthing is complete. They must be kept warm – a lamp would be useful in this instance. It takes up to 6 hours for all the piglets to be born and a couple more for the two placentas to pass.

Newborn Old Spots keeping warm under a heat lamp

Newborn piglets will latch on to their mother's teats within minutes of being born and begin to suckle. This early milk is particularly rich: it contains colostrum, which is essential for the immediate development of the piglets' immune system. Once the piglets are feeding happily and the pen is clean and dry, you can leave them to it. But be on hand to check in every so often.

After 3–4 weeks of suckling, a 'creep feed' is gradually introduced. Feeding a small amount of solid food early on will help the piglets' transition from their mother's milk on to solid food and aid the gut and digestive development.

Your sow can have a second litter of piglets once the first litter has been weaned, although she must be given time to regain condition.

How many pigs should you keep?

Pigs are very social animals and enjoy each other's company. You should never keep one pig on its own: it will become frustrated, bored and lonely. A minimum of two pigs should be the order of the day – and these can give you a very plentiful supply of meat.

Two little pigs grow into two very big pigs quite quickly. If your animals 'kill out' at 90kg each, then, once all the blood and internal organs are removed, you could easily have two 70kg carcasses. In other words, keeping just two pigs could yield at least 140kg of pork. This quantity of meat will probably keep you and your family well fed for the best part of a year.

You might like to rear four pigs, and when it comes to slaughter, keep the meat from two and sell the rest. This could generate enough income to cover your feed bill as well as your initial outlay for the weaners themselves.

Selling home-reared pork

If you plan to sell any of your home-reared pork it will need to be butchered in a licensed cutting room. Your local abattoir should offer this service. As well as butchering your meat, they may also be able to process some of it into fresh sausages, ham and bacon that you can go on to sell. This can often make your home-reared pork more attractive to any prospective customer, as it means they get everything they want in the one box. However, I'd suggest you ask your abattoir or butcher about the recipes they use, as some commercial sausage seasonings can be full of E-numbers and strange colourings.

Bear in mind the logistics of selling your pork, too. You need to find the buyers, organise a cutting list (in which your prospective customer might like to have a say), arrange delivery or collection and make sure you get a fair price for your efforts. That's a lot of work, so try to make the process as simple as possible so it doesn't turn into a logistical quagmire. I'd certainly advise you to standardise the cuts you offer.

Slap mark tool

Arrange for your customers to pick up their pork punctually on the morning it is butchered, and operate a strict cash-on-collection mentality. You won't have room to refrigerate your customers' pork, so 'Can I pick it up tomorrow?' is out of the question.

Some legal facts

You must register the holding on which your pigs will be kept before you actually buy them. In order to do this, contact the RPA (Rural Payments Agency), an executive agency of DEFRA. It only takes a few minutes to register. They will post you your County Parish Holding number (CPH). This is a nine-digit number, such as 13/579/1113: the first two digits relate to the county your pigs are kept in, the next three to the parish and the last four are unique to the keeper.

You will need to arrange for a movement licence, or AML2, when you collect your new pigs. The person you are buying the pigs from will fill out their part, and on arrival at your holding, you must complete your section. A movement licence provides important traceability: DEFRA can see where the pigs are and where they have been. Once the pigs arrive on your holding, you won't be able to move them, or any other livestock, off your land for 21 days. This is called the '21-day standstill' and it protects against the rapid spread of disease.

Before your pigs arrive, speak with your local AHVLA office (Animal Health and Veterinary Laboratories Agency), giving them your CPH number as a reference. They will register you as a 'pig keeper' and send you your herd mark – one or two letters followed by four digits. Your unique DEFRA herd mark is kept on a single database and provides for simple and effective traceability. The AHVLA will send you a registration document, which will contain your personal details, CPH and herd mark. All this information is important and must be kept safely along with any movement records and identification documents.

You must identify your pigs by either a plastic or metal ear tag or slap mark. You can fit ear tags yourself with pig tag pliers. A slap mark tool will leave a permanent ink-based tattoo of your herd number on the skin of the pig. This can also be done by you at home quickly and simply. Without clear identification markings, pigs won't be accepted at an abattoir.

Choosing a Breed

We keep rare and traditional pig breeds at River Cottage.

They bring a huge amount of character to the farm and are a joy to see in the paddocks. Traditional breeds have bloodlines that can be traced back hundreds of years to a time before factory farming, when family-run, open-pasture farms and smallholdings were commonplace. Different breeds became known and loved for their individual characteristics, such as their size, colouring, conformation and temperament, and, more importantly, their excellent and unique flavours, textures and fat marbling.

These traditional breeds still deliver those wonderful qualities, but on the whole, they are not suitable for intensive commercial farming. There is no place for them in today's economy-driven, intensive pork industry. They simply cannot compete with our box-ticking commercial breeds and, as a result, some heritage-breed pigs are becoming extremely rare, while others are in danger of being lost forever.

It's important to consider carefully which breed of pig to buy, rare or otherwise. They are all different and all very appealing in their individual ways. However, some will suit you better than others. Ask yourself: What do I want from my pigs? Is it all about maximising the return on your investment and filling the freezer? In this case, you may well want a big, fast-growing pig, like the Large White. If, however, you're more interested in companionship, and how your pigs behave with your children, then a friendly, docile breed such as the Berkshire (sometimes called 'the lady's pig') is in order. If you want a pig with particularly large back legs for your prosciutto hams, a Tamworth might suit you. If, on the other hand, you're longing to cook the ultimate roast pork belly, a Large Black, with its long, well-streaked belly, fits the bill.

Some breeds take the term 'free-range' very much to heart and can be expected to make regular, concerted efforts to outdo your fencing. Have you got the patience for that? Other breeds are somewhat more contented, happy to remain within the security of their own paddock.

Common breeds of pig are bred in great numbers due to their suitability for large-scale pig farming. Such breeds include the Duroc, the Welsh, the British Landrace and the Large White. In the 1950s, pig farmers were advised that the best way to increase profitability was to focus on these breeds. Commercially, they are viable and reliable, offering the farmer, the retailer and the broader consumer the consistency they require. These pigs are long and lean, and far less hairy (and therefore easier to process) than the more traditional breeds. They also reach slaughter weight far quicker. The Landrace and Large White are intensively farmed in huge numbers across Britain and are the source of the bulk of fresh and processed pork available to us today.

However, the unfortunate consequence of this concentration on a few high-yielding breeds was a huge decline in our rare- and heritage-breed pigs. By the

Commercial pig farming

mid-seventies, the breeding populations of traditional pigs had plummeted. Prized breeds like the Berkshire, Gloucestershire Old Spot and Saddleback had reached dangerously low levels.

If you are buying pigs to raise at home, choosing a rare breed goes some way towards protecting it from extinction. But it also means you are far more likely to produce totally delicious pork. Before you decide on a pig breed, I would suggest taking a day out and making a simple piggy road trip. Visit a handful of small farms that have breeds of pig which interest you. You can see them for yourself that way. You can also speak to the pig keepers and find out what they consider appealing about their particular breed.

In this chapter I've outlined the main characteristics of each breed, in order to help you decide which is best for you. In addition, most rare breeds have their own society or club and the websites of these organisations will give you more in-depth information on the pig you have your eye on, as well as the opportunity to ask specific questions of experienced breeders. The British Pig Association (BPA), a long-established conservation body set up to safeguard pedigree bloodlines, is another excellent resource.

Berkshire

The Berkshire pig is dark in colour with white feet and a white patch on the face and tip of the tail. It has a relatively short snout and medium-sized pricked ears, and its dark skin affords it some protection from sunburn.

It is the oldest-recorded pedigree pig breed in Britain. Records dating back to the seventeenth century show that Cromwell's soldiers praised the quality of the hams and bacon from Berkshire pigs, as they passed through the county.

The popularity of the Berkshire declined thereafter and in 2008, when the emphasis was very much on producing 'white' pigs for bacon, only around 300 breeding sows were known to exist. However, I'm pleased to say that the breed has made an impressive recovery in recent years. The present-day Berkshire is smaller than its ancestors and has excellent characteristics. Its medium size and pleasant disposition make it an easy-to-manage breed, while its curious and friendly nature ensure it is a popular choice for many a pig keeper.

Today Berkshire meat is as highly revered as it was in Cromwell's era but not just in Britain – it is famous all over the world and widely celebrated by enthusiasts, farmers and chefs alike, who regard this dark, juicy, well-marbled pork as second to none. In Japan, Berkshire is considered the absolute pick of the pork. It is called kurobuta, meaning 'black hog', and valued in much the same way as their prime wagyu beef.

British Lop

This fine-looking pink pig hails from Devon, not far from River Cottage HQ. It has lived here quietly for centuries, firmly entrenched within the homesteads surrounding the Tavistock area. It went largely unnoticed as a breed by farmers further afield.

On first sight, the British Lop looks very much like a conventional pig – similar to the Landrace or the Welsh, two of our most common pink pigs – but it is most definitely a traditional breed, and a rare one at that. Originally registered and known as the National Long White Lop Eared breed, its name was shortened to the British Lop in the 1960s.

Dubbed and renowned for its large droopy ears, the British Lop is a popular choice for butchers and retailers who value traditional pork breeds. This is due both to its well-muscled, lean carcass and its light, sparse bristles – the latter gaining it favour within abattoirs as an easy-to-process rare breed. Hardy, manageable and docile, with good mothering qualities, it is valued by pig keepers too.

The British Lop is one of the few rare-breed pigs that will tolerate slightly more intensive forms of production. The pigs do pretty well in larger herds and they become accustomed to well-bedded straw barns more readily than many other breeds. They are valued for their efficiency in converting the food they eat into fine-quality meat, which makes them economical to keep.

Gloucestershire Old Spot

Originating from the shores of the River Severn in the Southwest, this breed is very well known in Britain, and has become a favourite of smallholders everywhere. Large, deep-bodied pigs with large lop ears, Gloucestershire Old Spots have distinctive black spots on their light coats. They are sometimes called 'orchard pigs', as they were commonly seen grazing in apple and pear orchards throughout the county, feeding on windfalls at the same time. In fact, legend has it that their spots are bruises left by falling apples.

The GOS is a very good forager and has the advantage that it is a particularly hardy breed and copes well in colder climes or where the weather tends to fluctuate to extremes. Often described as docile, these pigs have a gentle nature and make good mothers, as well as reliable breeding stock. They are good all-rounders, producing fine pork and excellent bacon, and the quality of their meat is celebrated by those in the know.

This fabulous pig has been awarded protected status or a 'Traditional Speciality Guarantee'. A TSG is a certification within the European Protected Food Names Scheme, which recognises the product's unique and traditional eating qualities. The designation is awarded irrespective of where the pigs are produced. However, to achieve this status, all Gloucestershire Old Spot pigs must be pedigree and they must be kept in high-welfare, non-intensive conditions.

Large Black

This breed, also known as the Devon Black, is instantly recognisable, thanks to the pigs' huge pointy lop ears which run right down to their snouts and almost cover their eyes completely. They have long deep bodies and have always been considered good pigs for fresh pork and bacon.

The Large Black is a hardy pig of good size, so it is well suited to traditional outdoor systems within a wide variety of climates. It is Britain's only all-black pig, but its coloration doesn't make it particularly popular, as many people do not like the dark patches and hair on their pork and bacon. The upside is that its skin pigmentation helps to prevent sunburn, and as a consequence, it became a popular pig to export to sunnier countries in the early 1900s.

Its powerful jowls and snout make the Large Black a renowned forager. It is also able to convert less than perfect grazing into body weight far more efficiently than some other pig breeds. And, despite its generous proportions, this pig's placid nature allows it to be settled: two strands of electric fence are plenty to keep this pig within the paddock.

Large Blacks are excellent mothers that produce good-sized litters and are able to keep them well fed. According to the *Guinness Book of Records*, a Large Black sow from Warwickshire held the title amongst all pigs for the largest number of litters, totalling 26 in a 12-year period.

Middle White

This medium-sized pig was registered as an official breed in 1852. A Yorkshire-based weaver successfully crossed his Large White sows with Small White boars (a breed that became extinct) and went on to enter them into the local agricultural show as Large Whites. They were subsequently rejected due to their small size but noted as a fine breed in their own right. The Middle White proved a popular pig to keep in Britain through the nineteenth and twentieth centuries. In the 1930s the Japanese emperor insisted on importing the Middle White, as this was the only pork he would eat.

In London the breed was known as 'the London Porker' as the meat could be cut into small joints, which were preferred by customers in the early part of the twentieth century.

Its slightly bat-like features make this pig instantly recognisable. It has pricked ears and a squashed snout set on a rather round face. This particular porker may be less inclined to root but is well suited to pasture grazing.

I've always been impressed with the quality of the Middle White carcass. Its manageable size makes it easy to butcher at home while its well-set meat and clean white fat make for wonderful fresh pork cuts, which roast beautifully, but will also cure very well too. As a suckling pig, it is renowned for roasting whole, producing succulent, flavourful meat.

Oxford Sandy and Black

We've had much success keeping this good-natured, pretty pig at River Cottage. It is one of our favourites, and I'm pleased to say it is increasing in popularity. In the late 1980s numbers were so low that it was considered to be near extinction.

OSBs originate from Oxford, as their name suggests, and are one of our oldest varieties of native pig. They have historical connections to the Tamworth and Berkshire, which is evident in their distinctive coloration. Their chestnut-red coats are splashed with black, which has earned them the nickname 'the plum pudding pig'. Personally, I think this has a lovely ring to it – I've always loved roast pork with plums.

A hardy, well-natured breed, the Oxford Sandy and Black is very well suited to mixed outdoor conditions, but it will also function happily under a variety of management systems. Its characteristics certainly make it an appropriate choice for someone starting out in pig keeping.

Medium- to large-sized, this semi-lop-eared porker has great conformation. Its strong legs produce sizeable hams and its long, deep body will give a good length to the loin and breadth to the belly. I would say that a well-fed, happy OSB produces some of the finest pork for the kitchen. The meat is firm and well marbled and hangs well. And these pigs put on a good layer of fat, which means their meat makes excellent charcuterie as well.

Saddleback

I'm particularly fond of the Saddleback. It was the first rare-breed pig I really had the pleasure of getting to know – both as a hardy outdoor forager enjoying the space of the River Cottage paddock and as a firm-set, well-marbled carcass on which I cut my butcher's teeth.

The British Saddleback was first established as a breed in its own right in the late 1960s. It's a cross of two similar pigs: the Essex and the Wessex Saddlebacks. These breeds had very similar markings: black and white, with a continuous belt of white hair circling the shoulders and forelegs. The Essex was often touted as 'the gent's pig', being considered fancier, whilst the workaday Wessex pig was 'the farmer's choice'.

Today's large lop-eared Saddleback still retains the classic coloration of its forebears, as well as occasionally having white hind feet and a white tip to the tail. It is a hardy and well-built breed, with a good foraging ability and a docile nature. Within organic pork production, it has built a fine reputation for its meat – both pork and bacon.

The Saddleback makes a very good mother. She is not overly fussy or intense but instead just prefers to get on with it in her own natural way. She produces plenty of milk for her litter and will tend to her young despite the cold, the rain and the wind.

Tamworth

This wonderful ginger pig originated in Tamworth, Staffordshire, during the early 1800s. It's a long-looking, leggy pig with a fine frame, a drawn-out snout and tidy, pricked ears. The colour of its thick bristles ranges from a light ginger to darker red. Bold and lively with plenty of personality, it is sometimes referred to as an aristocratic pig.

Like many other traditional breeds, the number of Tamworths fell dangerously low after the Second World War, as farmers were persuaded to concentrate their efforts on faster-growing, more economical breeds. It is thanks to the hard work of a handful of dedicated breeders that the Tamworth pig – along with many other traditional breeds – has survived.

Tamworths are closely related to our early indigenous forest-dwelling pigs, which makes them hardy, rugged creatures that do extremely well in colder conditions. They love woodland, bracken and scrub and their powerful snouts make them great foragers. They will turn over rough ground with ease, which makes them particularly appealing to keen gardeners.

The slow-maturing Tamworth is a great 'dual purpose' pig, producing well-set pork for roasting and grilling, as well as excellent hams and bacon. In controlled taste tests carried out by Bristol University, Tamworth pork was ranked as more delicious than a host of other rare breeds.

Land, Fencing
& Housing

Unlike us, pigs don't ask for much to keep them happy, but they do ask to be kept outside. Pigs love to be outdoors: British rare-breed pigs are literally born to it. These hardy creatures have a strong natural instinct to stand on earth and grass, beneath the sun and sky. They are curious, clever and playful animals, and they enjoy rooting and foraging for food. They like space to run and dodge with their siblings, a cool place to wallow when it's hot and, of course, somewhere clean and dry to shelter and sleep.

Adequate space and housing should be one of your first considerations and at the forefront of your mind when you are deciding whether to keep pigs or not. All the preparations will have to be made prior to your pigs arriving. It's worth giving yourself plenty of time to think it through carefully and get things just so: 'To be financially successful at raising hogs primarily requires the ability to think like a hog.' Louis Bromfield, *From My Experience* (1955).

The land or paddock

Pigs don't need acres of space. The bottom of a large garden or the corner of a small field will be more than adequate. At River Cottage our pig paddocks are about 20 x 20 metres, giving our pigs 400 square metres of space, which is sufficient for them to run around. Exercise keeps them strong and healthy – in both body and mind. We keep four animals in a paddock this size, giving them an average of 100 square metres each. We could keep six, but we find the pasture does better for longer with two less snouts and eight less trotters at work.

Your pig paddock needn't be tidy. By nature, pigs are inquisitive rummagers and love nothing more than a rough old patch of twisted, overgrown brambles and weed. Uneven grassy tufts bring variety underfoot and a few logs or stumps offer something to tussle and barge.

You certainly won't need to prepare the ground for them. In fact, they'll make short work of any green pasture, tilling the earth like bionic rotavators. Once your pigs have gone on to a better place, their vacant patch will be the perfect spot for you to establish a vegetable garden: weed-free and rich in manure. A symbiotic circle can begin.

Shade is an important consideration when picking a spot for your pigs to live. They must be able to get out of direct sunshine. Many breeds of pig, particularly those with light skin, will burn if they are exposed to too much sun, in exactly the same way that we do. Shade can be achieved naturally be way of trees and broad hedge lines or created by you in the form of a well-constructed canopy. Either way it's an essential component of a considered housing scheme and one that must not be overlooked.

Pigs harbour a primal attraction to woods and woodland. Their ancestors were forest dwellers, skulking and charging over the soft, truffly earth. If you have access to a small area of woodland or copse and you can feasibly incorporate it into your pigs' paddock, then so much the better. They'll be happy as a pig in… woodland!

A good-sized paddock, stocked appropriately, should keep your pigs happy and healthy as long as you're not intending to keep them for more than a year, but the lie of the land and weather will come into play. If your paddock becomes overly muddy due to our less than predictable British climate, it will prove an inhospitable place for your pigs to live. You will have to be prepared to move them to fresh ground for their own welfare.

If you're lucky enough to have acres to play with and the funds to felicitate, it is well worth creating two fenced paddocks at the same time, even if you only intend to keep a few pigs each year. It will make the pigs' and your lives so much easier if you can let them move on to fresh pasture should you need to.

A paddock needs time to recover once your pigs have been sent to slaughter. We let ours stand for 6 months before more pigs are reared on it. This allows time for fresh pasture to shoot and reduces the possibility of the ground becoming 'pig sick' – a term used to describe a paddock that carries ground-based parasites, which can infect livestock on it.

Houses

There are various housing options for your pigs, none complicated or particularly expensive. The most important thing is to offer shelter from the elements. If you have any kind of fixed abode for them, such as a block-built sty, stable or sturdy shed, you're one step ahead. You might even have a hose, drainage and electricity. Of course, such luxuries aren't available to everyone, but don't worry: pigs have a modest sense of grandeur. The familiar, traditional dome-shaped pig ark – solidly constructed of corrugated galvanised metal – suits all but the pickiest porkers.

Arks come in various sizes, and your choice will be determined by how many pigs you intend to keep. They can be insulated for pigs living in colder climes, and they come with optional floors and doors – I recommend both. A sturdy wooden floor will keep your pigs and piglets dry in even the worst weather and a door with a latch can be invaluable should you need to keep your pigs inside for any reason.

If the traditional ark isn't for you, more aesthetically pleasing alternatives are available – everything from lovely wooden arks, which are warmer in the winter, and cooler in the summer, to models made from 100% recycled plastic, which I think are great and look much better than they sound. See the Directory (p.248) for a few good ark suppliers.

Of course, there is also always the option to build an ark yourself. If you do go down the DIY route, bear in mind that your pig house is going to have as much as 100kg rubbing up against it on a daily basis. It needs to be strong and durable.

Surprisingly, pig arks don't need to be especially big. A 2.5-square-metre ark can house five or six 'porkers' (60–70kg pigs being reared for fresh pork) or three to four 'baconers' (90–110kg pigs taken to a larger weight for bacon). But you must make sure the ark is big enough for you to get in and clean out on a regular basis. You won't want to be crawling around in mucky straw or constantly banging your head on the ceiling.

We clean our arks out every couple of weeks. The old bedding is removed, the floor swept out and the space is replenished with fresh, clean straw. Everything we take out goes on the compost heap, and in time it rots down to form a rich mulch.

Pigs hate being cold and wet: in such conditions, they'll be neither happy nor healthy and they will need more food in order to keep themselves warm. Whether your ark has a floor or not, all draughts should be sealed as best you can. Try to position your ark on higher ground within the paddock, where the earth will be more free-draining. You should also try to site arks so the entrance is facing away from the prevailing wind. Pigs hate a windy house. They like to 'nest' in dry, clean bedding, piling on top of each other as they do. So it's essential, as mentioned earlier, that their home is laid with plenty of fresh loose straw. More straw at the entrance to the ark will help keep the thoroughfare cleaner and drier.

Traditional corrugated-iron pig ark

Plastic pig ark

Barbed-wire fencing

Electric fencing

Using a pig board to herd pigs

Fencing

You may have spent weeks creating a piggy utopia with house and grounds, the envy of all your peers and their piggies, but choose inadequate fencing and you'll be the laughing stock(man) of the village.

Use either a good posted fence with sheep or pig netting or a decent electric fencing system. Both are suitable, provided they are strong and put in correctly. If a pig can get out, it will, so a slapdash approach to fencing is a total waste of time. Chasing pigs up and down in a desperate bid to secure them may be a comic spectacle for the onlooker, but it is actually a very stressful experience for both pig and keeper. And if a pig gets on to a busy road, it can spell disaster.

If you opt for a traditional posted fence, span the base with two strands of barbed wire. This stops the pigs pushing and snuffling their way out. Make sure the wire is on the inside of the posts.

An electric fence has its pros and cons. Once a pig knows what it is, and what it does, it becomes an effective and portable option. Electric fencing allows you the freedom to strip-graze. This means fencing off an area of ground for your pigs to live on, then once this area has been accordingly 'turned over' by the pigs, you can move them to fresh new ground. Electric fencing makes this process practical and manageable. Pigs will quickly learn that an electric fence, however insignificant it seems to them physically, is a fence nonetheless. They are so smart that one or two encounters with their perimeter marker will give them the gist of it.

You'll need to fit a gate of sorts for access in and out of the paddock. Never underestimate your pigs' strength. A big animal can easily lift a gate clean off its hinges; flipping the top hinge over and rehanging the gate will stop such antics.

Ideally, your gate will be big enough to get your vehicle and trailer through. If it is only big enough to allow your pigs in and out, then you'll need a sensible solution for loading the pigs into the trailer when the time arrives.

When it comes to guiding a pig from one place to another, a 'pig board' can be very handy. These are used as an aid for encouraging the pigs to go where you want them to. The problem is that if pigs can see through a space, they may well try to physically get through it, so solid boards of this kind are evident when pigs are shown at country fairs.

Feeding & Health

We are what we eat and this is absolutely true for pigs too. But don't worry, with a little time and effort you'll be able to provide your pigs with an excellent mixed diet that will keep them healthy and happy.

Your pigs will need feeding twice every day – in the morning and later on in the afternoon – and must have access to fresh water at all times. If you're not able to be there at feeding time, you must find someone reliable and trustworthy to feed your pigs for you. It's not optional, but it's easy enough to get into the swing of a pig-feeding schedule – and very rewarding. Pigs favour routine and they will be ready to meet you, each time you come round the corner with feed bucket in hand, at about the same time every day.

Dry feed

Pigs love to eat, yes indeed. But, as with everything, excess is not a good thing. A very fat pig may not be a healthy pig. There is a limit to how much you should allow your pigs to gorge. As a rule, you shouldn't give a grown pig any more than 2.5kg dry feed a day – less if it's being mixed with vegetables, fruit and other fodder. We feed our young pigs 400–500g food each day, increasing to a total of 2.5kg per day when fully grown.

The chart below explains this. During the first and second months the piglet should be suckling with its mother, so unless you're breeding piglets, you won't need to worry about this period. After the seventh month you would continue to feed a maximum of 2.5 kg per day until the pig was slaughtered.

DRY FEED QUANTITIES

3rd month	4th month	5th month	6th month	7th month
500g per day	1kg per day	1.5kg per day	2kg per day	2.5kg per day

At River Cottage we feed our pigs organic pig nuts – a natural, dry pellet-based feed that is high in protein and essential minerals. Our young pigs get a weaner/grower feed, which they seem very keen on, and after several months progress to a grower/finisher feed. Organic pig feeds are free from GM ingredients, growth promoters and other unnecessary additives. We strongly believe that pigs should be allowed to grow naturally and normally.

We use a company called the Organic Feed Company, which provides a range of feeds made from 100% organically grown ingredients for a variety of animals, including poultry, goats, sheep, cattle and, of course, pigs. These feeds have full Soil Association approval, ensuring quality and traceability throughout.

Other food

Frustratingly, it is illegal to feed your pigs anything that has been into your kitchen, or any kitchen, because of the risk of contamination from raw or cooked meat. This law, which applies even in vegetarian households, was introduced in 2001 in an attempt to limit the spread of diseases, including foot and mouth disease and swine fever.

Unfortunately, this ban has economic and environmental implications, as we are giving up more and more land to grow livestock feed crops every day. It's an issue that needs addressing. We waste a third of all the food produced in the world today, which is an awful statistic. If it's processed and monitored in the correct way, food waste could be safely fed to pigs instead of going to landfill, thereby reducing the need for cultivated animal feed crops. All this said, feeding your pigs kitchen scraps is simply not an option at the moment.

However, it is still possible to supplement your pigs' diet with fresh produce. At River Cottage, much of our fresh salad and vegetable preparation takes place outside rather than in the kitchen – you can do the same. You can feed your pigs fruit and veg that has come direct from your garden or an allotment.

Alternatively, you may be able to come to an arrangement with a friendly farm shop or greengrocer that needs to get rid of fruit, vegetables and salad past their best. If they can't sell this produce, they may be happy to part with it for free – or for a nominal sum (half a kilo of sausages later in the year perhaps?).

Such gleanings provide pigs with a veritable feast and the variety needed in a well-rounded diet. Surprisingly, some pigs can be fussy eaters but on the whole they will be more than happy to be offered fresh fruit, veg and trimmings.

Offer your pigs any of the following:
- Leek tops
- Greens, such as chard and spinach
- All brassicas
- Courgettes, marrows and aubergines
- Tomatoes and cucumbers
- Apples, pears and plums
- Salad leaves, bolted lettuce and flowering herbs
- Beetroot tops
- Woody radishes, plus their tops
- Turnips
- Stringy beans, gone-over peas (pods and all)
- Sweetcorn
- Carrots

Do not give your pigs:
- Parsnip leaves – they can irritate the pig's mouth
- Raw potatoes in quantity – they will upset their stomachs
- Raw onions – they can be too strong
- Citrus fruits – they are too bitter for them in most cases
- Rhubarb leaves – they can be poisonous to pigs and people
- Meat or any meat-based products of any description
- Any food that has been in your kitchen

Pigs love cow's milk and whey, and will be pretty happy quaffing it straight. On colder mornings, you can give it to them warm as porridge with a little barley meal, milled wheat, corn or oats. In some cases, too much milk can upset their stomachs but, unless you live on a dairy farm, it's unlikely you'll have access to enough excess milk to make it a problem.

Combined with the assortment of insects, worms, bark, grass, roots, flowers and weeds that any free-ranging pig will snuffle up for themselves, these various sorts of fodder will give you happy, well-nourished animals.

Feeding troughs

It is important to give your pigs a sturdy trough to eat from. It will keep most of the food off the ground, most of the time, which is good – particularly in wet conditions. Setting the trough on a hard surface will make things easier for the pigs as they gather to eat: half a dozen paving slabs set on to the ground should keep things nicely in order. Don't be surprised if your pigs knock over or roll the trough from time to time – as long as it's well built, no harm should be done.

Drinking

Pigs should have access to fresh water at all times, so think about the most practical way to provide this facility before you install your animals. If your paddock is close to a water main, you can rig up an automatic drinker: this will be clean, economical and efficient – but not much fun for the piggies. A simple galvanised trough, on the other hand, will keep your pigs' thirst quenched but also offer them hours of aqua fun. Flipping their drinking trough in order to create a glorious mud wallow might become a familiar scene on warmer days – and one mustn't begrudge pigs such simple pleasures. Do expect your daily routine to involve righting, cleaning and refilling their drinking trough.

Health

There will always be diseases and ailments that can affect your pigs. As with raising any livestock – including children – prevention is the key. Good practice aligned with fresh air, sunshine, freedom to carry out natural behaviour, shelter, nutritious feed, fresh pasture, variety in the diet, clean water and managed sanitation will contribute enormously to the wellbeing of your animals.

Good hygiene should always be practised across the board by you and anyone else who comes to visit your pigs, particularly if they've come from another farm. Always wash your hands with antibacterial soap after handling your animals. And it's essential to find a good vet who has experience with pigs and smallholders at your level. Their input and wisdom will be invaluable should your pigs become sick.

The twice-daily feeding is a vital opportunity to check your pigs over and also to just *be* with them. It's no good just lobbing the food and turning tail. Take time to watch them, listen to them and give them a scratch or a pat. Being with your pigs is fundamental to their health. Unlike you, they can't pick up the phone and call the doctor when they're feeling poorly. Their only hope, if they are unwell, is that you notice it.

You don't have to be looking hard to realise when your pigs aren't themselves. There are some key signs, and at the top of that list is appetite. Has your pig lost interest in its food? Is its appetite not what it usually is? Is it being picky? Is it lying down when it would normally be up, chomping and romping with its siblings?

Dull, weeping eyes are another sign that all is not well. And, if the pig is lame, you'll notice a change in its gait: is it low or carrying itself differently? Listen out for shallow panting or coughing and feel for fever. If your pig seems hot it may be worth taking its temperature. Anything out of the ordinary warrants a closer look.

If you think your pig is sick, think practically and rationally. Carefully examine the animal. What exactly do you think is wrong with it? Make some notes and give your vet a call. Describing the symptoms will give your vet a better idea of what the trouble might be. It could be that medicine is required to treat the condition. The sooner you can treat your pig, the better the chances of it recovering to full health.

Many medicines and treatments have a withdrawal period after the completion of a course, during which the pig cannot be slaughtered. Your vet will advise you on this. You should keep records of what treatments have been administered and when.

Heat stroke and sunburn

These conditions should be guarded against from the outset, as they can cause your pigs a lot of discomfort. As suggested earlier, shade in the paddock should be one of your earliest considerations – you can't just rely on the pigs' ark as this can become hot and uncomfortable in the midday sun. Trees can provide good natural shade, but if there are none in the paddock, a strong awning or lean-to will suffice. In hot weather pigs will wallow in mud, which will help to keep the sun off their skin, provided you've made it possible for them to do so. And for those who didn't know, it is perfectly common for pig keepers to apply a sunscreen to their pigs' ears and other sensitive areas to protect them should it be deemed necessary.

Vaccinations and treatments

If you plan to keep a sow to breed piglets from, you'll need to be up to speed with the various treatments and vaccinations required to safeguard both her health and that of her piglets. And, if you are buying weaners to grow on for pork, make sure they have been vaccinated or treated against the main offenders I've listed below. It's always a good idea to consult your vet if you're not sure about something, even if that's with the simplest of concerns. They will be able to advise and support you, which will, in turn, make your pig keeping a more enjoyable pastime.

Enteritis This inflammation of the intestine can be caused by consuming food or water contaminated with bacteria or viruses. Breeders should vaccinate sows against enteritis before they farrow, which will protect the piglets from the disease.

Worms All piglets need worming, but you might not need to do this yourself if the breeder has already treated yours, especially if you only plan to keep them for 8–9 months. If you are unsure, or suspect your pigs might have worms, check with your vet as there are simple ways of testing.

Erysipelas This bacterial infection is one of the more common conditions found on smallholdings. It's carried by rats, mice and birds as well as sometimes being hidden in the soil. It manifests itself via raised, diamond-shaped areas on the pig's skin. In some cases, antibiotics can be an effective treatment but, if the condition is left unchecked, it can be fatal.

Lice If you notice your pigs scratching and rubbing like mad, it could be a sign of lice. On closer inspection, you should be able to see them. Treatment is available in the form of powders and injections. It's important to treat all your pigs and their housing, otherwise they can pick up the lice again.

Scour Fairly common in young piglets, scour or diarrhoea is not a disease as such, rather the repercussions of an upset stomach. More often than not, it's caused by E. coli. It can be fatal if untreated, as the piglets dehydrate quickly. Breeders should vaccinate their sows against scour as this protects the young. When you buy your weaners, check for any signs of scour. You don't want to take infected pigs home.

Checking the tail end of an Oxford Sandy and Black

Slaughter

You won't be surprised to read that taking your pigs to slaughter can be very difficult. Even the most old-hand pig farmers can be seen faltering with the latches on their trailers at the abattoir doors. It's perfectly natural to feel emotion. You've got to know your pigs; you're sure to be fond of them and their funny ways. There's no shame in the sadness their death brings, but it is important for you to consider the idea of slaughter with a rational stance from the outset. It's no good entering into 'project pig' if you can't handle the culmination of it: killing the animal and eating the meat.

I knew a good chef who kept a couple of pigs. He loved the process of rearing them – and the animals themselves. But he went to bits when the day of slaughter came around. He brought their carcasses home and put them in the bathtub. Grieving, he went off the rails, drinking hard for several days. He hadn't prepared himself for the very thing he had set out to do.

Nearly all the chefs at River Cottage have accompanied pigs to slaughter at some stage. It's important for them to witness this: they will have watched the piglets grow since their arrival. Understanding the process of slaughter is very much part of what we do, how we learn and how we teach people about food and cooking. For my chefs and me, this is the point at which pigs become pork and a new journey begins, away from the paddock and sty and into the heat, salt and sage.

From a practical point of view, the day of slaughter is nothing to panic about. The process is quite straightforward and only takes an hour or so. As long as you are organised and confident, it should go without a hitch. Poor planning, on the other hand, can lead to trouble: a stressed pig, an upset keeper and a scowling slaughterman… a disappointing scenario all round.

When to slaughter

It can be tricky to know exactly when to send your pigs to slaughter. Usually the time is determined via a combination of the animal's age, weight and condition and, ultimately, what you want to do with the meat.

There are three recognised terms describing a pig's size and condition. A 'porker' is a pig brought up to 'pork weight' – normally about the 65kg mark – in order to produce lean fresh pork joints. Pigs can achieve this weight in just 4–5 months.

A 'baconer' is a pig grown primarily for bacon and charcuterie rather than for fresh cuts and is slaughtered at 8–9 months of age, when it will have laid down more fat, regularly killing out at 80–100kg. We nearly always bring our pigs on to this sort of size.

A 'cutter' describes a pig brought to a weight somewhere between a porker and a baconer, giving larger but possibly fattier fresh joints.

Weighing your pig

There is a simple way of working out the rough weight of your pig. All you have to do is note down a few vital statistics and apply a basic formula. You can use a piece of string to take the measurements, or a tailor's tape measure. Firstly note the girth of your pig (just behind the shoulders) in metres. Then measure the length from the base of its tail to the centre of its head, just between the ears.

The formula is girth x girth x length x 69.3. So, say you have a baconer with a girth of 1.24 metres and a length of 1.05 metres. The sum would be as follows:

1.24 x 1.24 x 1.05 x 69.3 = 112

Your pig will weigh roughly 112kg.

Of course, you can't just roll up and weigh any old pig like this. If they don't know or trust you, you may well be bitten for trying such a thing. Your own pigs shouldn't be too offended though, provided you make a fuss of them with some food beforehand.

Taking your pig to the abattoir

At Park Farm, we make sure our pigs are booked in with Trevor at our local abattoir, Snells, 2–3 weeks in advance. It's close to the farm, professionally run and we trust Trevor and his team with the animals we send there.

I would recommend finding out about the slaughterhouse you intend to use. Pay a visit, introduce yourself and ask questions. Some abattoirs can be reluctant to take rare breeds because their hairier skins can take much longer to process. Make sure the slaughterhouse won't have a problem with your pigs. Then, if you have a good feeling about the set-up, let them know that you'll be booking your pigs in with them at some stage in the future. It will cost you around £20–30 to have your pig slaughtered but this can go up or down slightly, depending on the weight of the pig.

Make a clear note of the date and time your animals are due to go to slaughter then, several days in advance, start getting your pigs used to the trailer you plan to transport them in. If your pigs have never seen it before, they might be reluctant to step inside, so put the trailer in the paddock and feed them inside it. This ensures they will be more than happy to walk in and out. A trailer is a significant investment so you might want to think about hiring or borrowing one first time around.

It's essential that your trailer is roadworthy, nice and clean inside and out, with fresh straw on the floor. Make sure you check it over thoroughly before transporting the pigs. It's not unheard of for them to chew tyres or pull at cables while getting used to a trailer.

The day before slaughter, give your pigs only a small amount of food in the morning. After that you shouldn't feed them again, so make it something they will really enjoy! Pigs should not have food in their stomachs when they are processed: eviscerating a full animal is not easy and the gut can burst and make a real mess. This can lead to the lovely offal being condemned.

Minimising any kind of stress prior to slaughter is of the utmost importance. Not only is this the humane approach, but it also leads to better-tasting meat. Stress stimulates the production of adrenaline, which can dramatically affect the flavour of your pig.

It might seem a good idea to load your pigs into the trailer the night before you take them to the abattoir. If they are used to it, they would bed down in there overnight, minimising any stress it might cause you and your pigs in the morning. But unfortunately this practice is illegal for welfare reasons.

However, if your pigs are accustomed to the trailer, they should follow you in as you shake the feed bucket. You could try leaving the trailer in their paddock with the tailgate down the night before: you may well find them happily asleep in there in the morning – the difference being that you're not shutting them in.

On the day

Set your alarm nice and early on the day of slaughter, as some abattoirs will call for the pigs from 7am. Make sure you have all the necessary paperwork, including your animal movement licence (AML2). If your smallholding is organic, you'll need to bring along the relevant documentation as well.

Make sure you know exactly where you have to go and where the holding bay at the abattoir is located. It is more than likely you'll have to reverse up to this (something worth practising if your trailer is new to you), and consider that if it's early, it may still be dark.

Don't take one pig on its own to slaughter if you can help it. Two pigs together will be far more comfortable in these unaccustomed circumstances. It's also important not to leave one pig on its own back at the paddock, as it will get lonely and frustrated.

If your pigs are held in a bay with lots of other pigs, fighting can break out. This is stressful for the pigs and should be avoided at all costs – another reason why it's worth asking questions at the slaughterhouse well ahead of time.

There will be a meat inspector or vet present and he or she will check your animals' health and general wellbeing on arrival. After you've dropped off your pigs, go into the office and let them know that you would like all your offal back. This will include the liver, lungs and heart as well as the spleen, caul fat and

The slaughter process

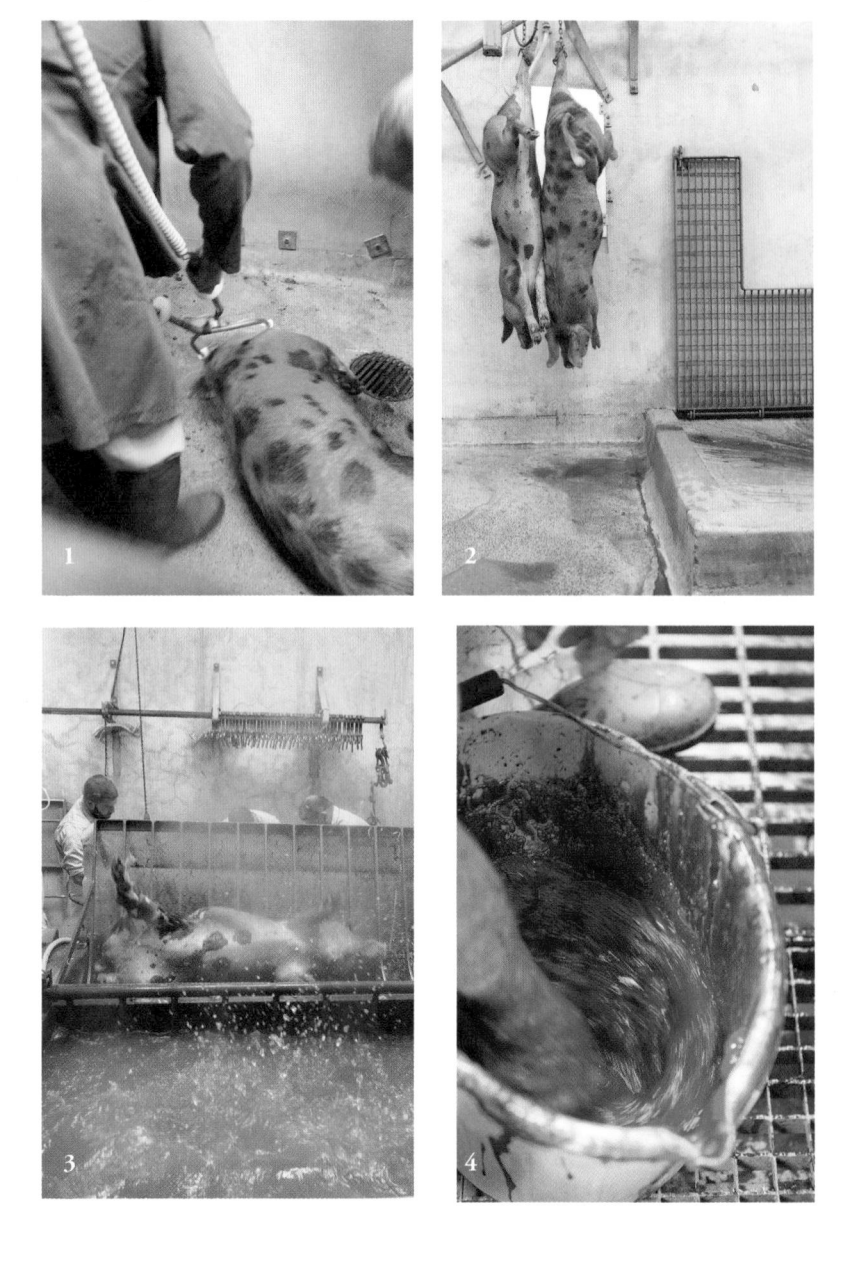

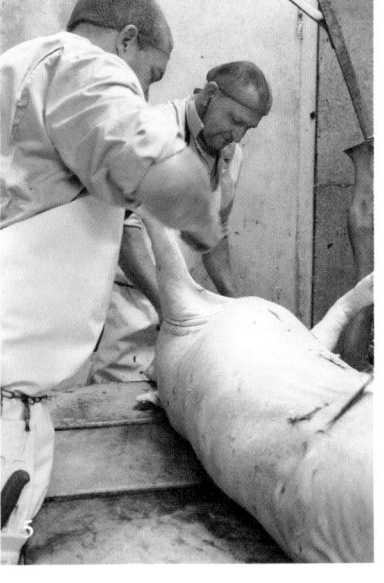

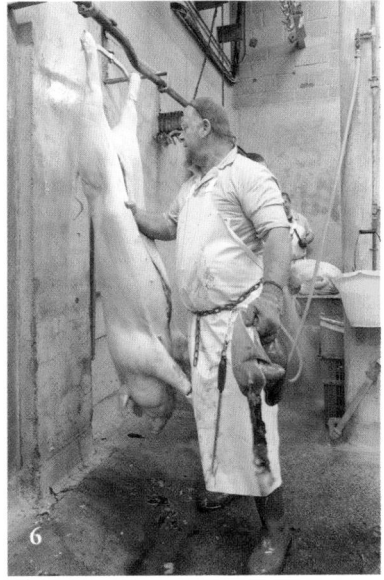

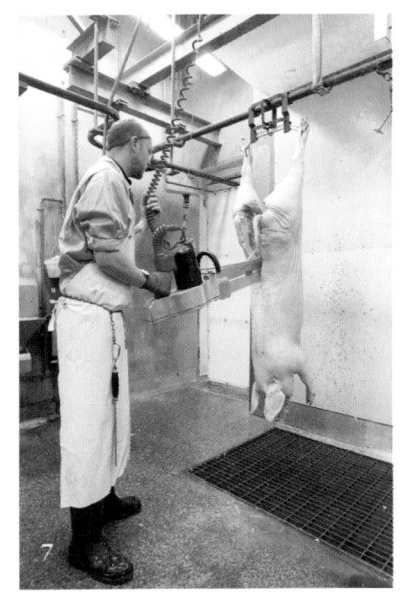

kidneys. If you intend to make black pudding, and I certainly hope you do, ask for the blood to be saved too. If possible, wait while your pigs are killed and collect the offal and blood straight away. It is essential for these products to be used very fresh.

The killing procedure should be quick, humane and completely stress-free for the animal. Generally, pigs are stunned by an electrical current (p.76, pic 1), which takes effect instantly, then hung up by the hind legs (pic 2), stuck and bled (pic 3), before being de-haired (pics 4 and 5) and eviscerated (pic 6). The carcass is split in two (pic 7) and thoroughly washed before being chilled (pic 8). Sometimes the head is left on, either split or left whole on one side of the carcass. I prefer the latter option – it's worth asking the abattoir if this is possible. The vet or inspector will check the processed carcass and offal for any sign of disease. Occasionally offal can be condemned and, if this is the case, the abattoir will notify you and tell you why.

If you can't pick up the offal on the day of slaughter, get it as soon as you can. The 'pluck', as it is called, comprises the lungs, heart and liver, and is removed in its entirety. Make sure the pluck you get is from your pig – they all look pretty similar.

Let the abattoir know when you will be back to collect the carcass. They will have the facilities to hang your pork for at least 3 days. This hanging time is not so much to mature the pork as with beef or lamb, but more to allow it to 'set' properly so it is firm and easy to work with.

The emotional response

Being confronted by a dead pig for the first time is quite a dramatic experience and all the more poignant if it's your own pig, to which you've devoted so much care and attention. You may go through a series of emotions that make tackling the task at hand tricky. Your turmoil may be short-lived or it may linger. That largely depends on your predisposition, but although it's a sad event, you will get over it.

I must confess, the first time I encountered a whole dead pig I was somewhat taken aback. I'd been asked to cook one over a wood fire at a village fete. I suppose that, as consumers, we are just not used to seeing whole dead animals, intact and lifeless with feet, eyes and tails. I struggled to get to grips with this unwieldy 70kg mass, because for me, as for many people, manhandling substantial deceased animals was not everyday stuff. But by the time it was mounted up on the spit, scored and seasoned, I'd already started to feel more comfortable and was at ease with the form lunch was taking.

Coming to terms with slaughtering your own pigs will never be straightforward but you will get used to the emotions involved. It's certainly a comfort to know that your animals will have led a far more enjoyable and natural life than the majority of pigs being slaughtered each day.

Butchery

You have two options when it comes to butchering your pig. Either you collect your pork, take it home and cut it up yourself, or you have someone do it for you.

Most good abattoirs will provide a butchery service, or occasionally a local butcher or travelling butcher may help out. Our abattoir does a 'farmer's cut', consisting of big primal joints such as whole legs, shoulders, bellies and loins, or possibly halves thereof. They also provide 'family cuts' for the freezer, which involves cutting the primal joints into smaller ones. Some of these can be boned and rolled, chops can be cut and some meat can be minced. You may be able to give your abattoir a cutting list of sorts, explaining precisely how you would like your pork to be prepared.

You will, of course, incur a small fee for these services but the going rate is reasonable, in my view. For an 80kg pig, a farmer's cut will cost in the region of £20, and family cuts £25–£30.

Striking up a relationship with an independent butcher may pay dividends when it comes to processing your own pigs. You should get a more thorough service from a local butcher because he should have the facilities and time to cater for your exact needs. He should be able to make bacon and hams for you, as well as fresh sausages and all the other specified cuts and joints you would like. It might even be that you can observe the butchering process if he is in agreement.

Having your animal butchered for you is a convenient and simple way of dealing with your pigs, post-life. Neat, labelled, bagged joints and cuts can be dropped effortlessly into the deep freeze. You won't need to even think about reaching for the knife until you're ready to cook them, and then it may only be to open the bag they came in. For some people, this is the only practical way to deal with the pork, particularly if they are killing several pigs at once. Lifestyle, time, space, knowledge and confidence all have to be weighed up at this point.

Butchery at home

Butchering your own pork is great fun, perfectly achievable, wonderfully rewarding and ultimately holistic. It's such a big piece of the smallholding jigsaw that it would be a shame not to experience the process at least once. It's amazing how much you can learn about pork and pork cookery by cutting up a carcass yourself. Literally everything from the snout through to the tail can be eaten or utilised in one way or another. It's an adventure that has limitless possibilities and outcomes, although it is understandably daunting for the beginner. If you intend to butcher your own pigs, a certain amount of practical preparation should be carried out, so that when the day comes, you're ready to tackle them head-on, so to speak.

Any hands-on butchery experience you can gain prior to working on your own pigs will be invaluable so, if the opportunity arises, grasp it with two hands. You may be able to book yourself on to a pig butchery course, which will give you a sound understanding of the basics, but attending special classes is not essential. You'll be able to gain the confidence and know-how you need to tackle your first pig from the pages of this book.

It would be a mistake to pick up your pigs late on a Monday afternoon if you've got a parents' evening to attend and you're off on business the following day. You need time and space to do the best job. I've always been charmed by the concept of a 'Pig Weekend' – a gathering of knives and minds centred around, but not solely limited to, the butchery and processing of your pigs. As well as being busy and structured, a weekend like this can be a veritable celebration of life, of food, of friends and family.

A weekend also gives you the time you need to produce not only recognisable joints ready for the freezer but a wide array of other gastronomic delights as well. You'll have time to make your own sausages, prepare terrines, cure bacon and render lard. Because two pigs yield such a vast volume of fresh pork, this two-day double-pronged approach is essential if you have a pair of animals, particularly if you don't have the facilities to refrigerate this much meat. But with adequate freezer space, and by utilising the magic of salt curing, you will have no problem dealing with every last bit of pork there is.

Butchery tools

Some friends of mine bought a house in a nearby village a few years ago. While clearing out the attic, they found a very old set of butcher's tools wrapped up in a leather apron: a few well-used knives, an old wooden-handled cleaver, a butcher's saw and steel, as well as some hooks. It made me think about the history of that set of tools and the butcher who had owned them. Within the folds of this apron was everything needed for the man's daily work, week upon week, year upon year.

To cut up your pigs – or any carcass for that matter – only a few tools are essential: two sharp knives, a sharpening steel, a butcher's saw and a meat cleaver will suffice. At Park Farm we also have a chunky butcher's block, which is great to work on but quite an effort to clean. Once used, it has to be scrubbed with a stiff wire brush that takes off the very top layer of wood. I have the utmost respect for butchers, who typically do this twice a day.

You are unlikely to have a butcher's block at home but a sturdy kitchen table will be more than adequate as a surface for your butchery. If you're worried about cutting into it, then top it with a suitably sized piece of clean plywood.

Butcher's saw

Meat cleaver

Boning knife

Steak knife

Other butchery equipment

If you plan to make your own sausages, you'll need a mincer and a sausage stuffer, which are both easy to source online. As with most things, the cheapest ones might not last that long or perform as well as the more durable, higher-priced alternatives.

These items of equipment come in a variety of shapes and sizes. Mincers range from the traditional crank-handled version, which clamps to your kitchen table and is available from most good car boots, through to big commercial powerhouses designed for large-volume processing. You will need to choose a machine that suits your own requirements, but most importantly you'll need to keep the blade good and sharp.

The same is true of sausage stuffers. They can be big or small, horizontal or vertical, electric or man-powered. Choose one that will cope with the amount of sausages you plan to make. That said, I'm no stranger to a funnel and the handle of a wooden spoon when push has come to shove.

Things that you'll find useful on the day:
- Table for cutting up the pig
- Boning knife – this will be the knife you use most of the time
- Steak knife for making big cuts, and slicing steaks and chops
- Steel for keeping your knives sharp
- Butcher's saw for sawing through bone
- Meat cleaver for dividing joints
- Meat hooks to hang joints on
- Mincer for mincing the meat for sausages, etc.
- Sausage stuffer for filling your sausages and salami
- Pestle and mortar for bashing up spices
- Mixing bowls for various tasks; have several to hand
- Ham crock or large plastic tubs for wet-curing hams, hocks and other cuts
- Large, deep plastic boxes for dry-curing hams
- Large and small freezer bags for bagging up your butchered cuts of pork
- Ball of butcher's string for tying up joints
- Stanley knife or a heavy craft knife for scoring the tough skin of a pig for crackling
- Tray to hold your knives, saw and steel

Butchery preparation

Assemble your kit in advance and decide where you're going to cut up the pigs. Then, when they arrive back from the abattoir, you're ready to go straight away.

In late autumn and early winter, it may be possible, and indeed preferable, to butcher your pig outside. As long as there are no flies about and it's not too warm, this can be a good place to do it and it may be more practical than swamping the kitchen with dozens of cuts of pork.

The golden rules:
- Keep your working area tidy. Have a bowl of hot soapy water at hand and a couple of clean dry tea towels.
- Keep your knives, saw and steel in one place, on a tray out of the way.
- Check that your knives and saw blade are sharp – this is very important, as having sharp knives will make things so much easier for you.
- Make confident clean cuts in straight lines, either vertically or horizontally.
- Every few minutes pass your knife over the steel to keep an edge on it – this will make the job much, much easier.
- Use your knife to cut through flesh and the saw to cut through bone.
- Have somewhere nearby where you can place your cuts of pork. If you have help on the day, which is always useful, the joints can be bagged up and labelled as you cut them.
- Get the butchery out of the way before you start making your sausages, bacon and pâtés.
- As soon as you have prepared a joint, refrigerate it.
- Remember not to freeze any cuts you would like to eat fresh.

Preparing the carcass

Lay the carcass, cut side up, on the surface you have chosen to butcher on and familiarise yourself with the anatomy of your pig. Identify the cuts you know well, like the belly, loin and hock.

Before any major cuts are made, I like to remove any spots of blood, membrane or sinew that seem out of place or unappetising, together with the eyeballs, which will be more or less the only real waste from the carcass. You will find the majority of this trim will come from the area where the pig was stuck and bled. Do your best to clear this up – getting rid of the blood will help keep the meat fresher for longer.

If your pig feels a little sticky to the touch, it may mean it's been hanging for too long in a fridge where the conditions are less than ideal. It may even be in the early stages of decay. Watch out for this when your pig comes back from the abattoir and report back if necessary. Hanging fridges are designed to age meat through managed temperature and humidity; if these are not right it won't dry properly.

Removing the tongue

On occasion, the tongue will be left in the pig's head. At other times you may find it attached to the offal, or the 'pluck' as it is termed. If it is still in the mouth of the pig it's best to remove it from the back.

Use the tip of the knife to carefully cut the tongue at the very base, where it is connected to the upper base of the throat (pic 1), to remove it completely from the head (pic 2). You can use the tongue in a classic brawn (see p.178) or pickle it in brine and serve it with lentils and salsa verde (see p.176).

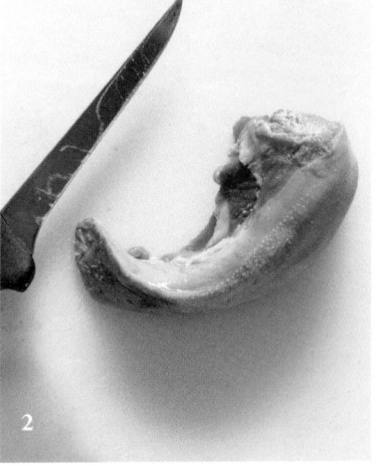

Removing the head

If the whole head is connected to one half of the pig, start on that half. Make a cut in line with the cut back edge of the top cheek. Saw through the spine, then make a long cut with a steak knife (pic 1). Set the head aside (pic 2) for later (see p.119).

Removing the kidney

Simply nick the point at which it is connected with the tip of your knife (pic 1) and it will come away easily (pic 2). Refrigerate or freeze the kidney for later.

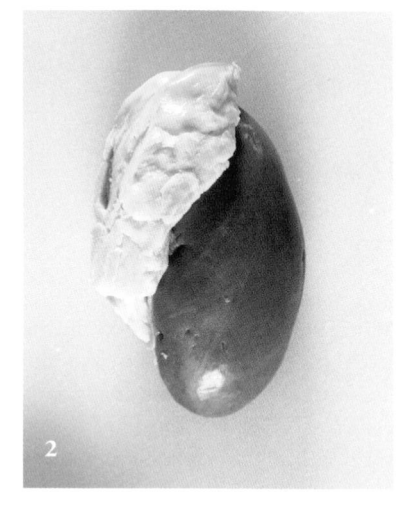

The primal cuts

When it comes to dividing up the main carcass I like to start by making three initial cuts. This will result in four different pieces of pork, the basic primal cuts. These primal cuts will be instantly recognisable to you as the shoulder, the loin, the belly and the leg. Very quickly what was once a big and possibly daunting carcass becomes but four simple joints that are manageable, familiar and full of possibility.

Key

1   Shoulder
2   Loin
3   Belly
4   Leg

Removing the shoulder

The ribs start in the centre of the shoulder. The first one is really quite small, but they get progressively bigger as they step out towards the belly.

Using the tip of a knife, make a shallow cut, or mark, between the fourth and fifth ribs (pic 1), from top to bottom. This initial cut will act as a guide. Now use the saw along this mark to cut through the bone (pic 2). Finish off with a clean long cut from the larger steak knife (pic 3) to separate the shoulder from the main carcass (pic 4).

Removing the leg

You will be able to see part of the pelvic bone at the top of the leg; this is called the aitch bone. You can use this bone as a guide for making the cut that separates the leg from the middle section of the pig.

Place two fingers next to the bone and make the cut just the other side of your fingers (pic 1). Use your knife to cut down to the bone, then use the saw to cut through the bone (pic 2). Finish the cut with the steak knife (pic 3) to separate the leg from the main carcass (pic 4).

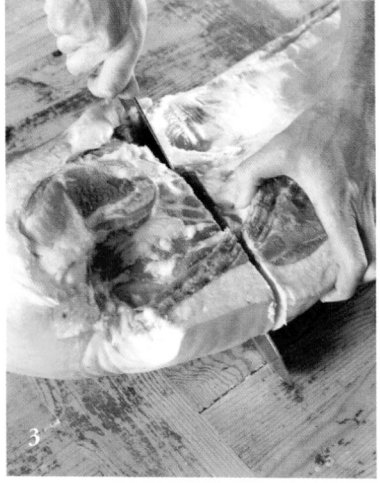

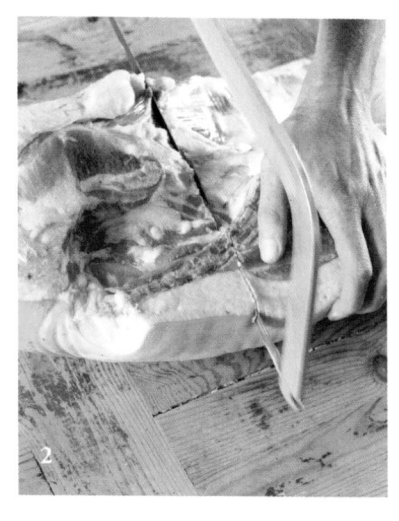

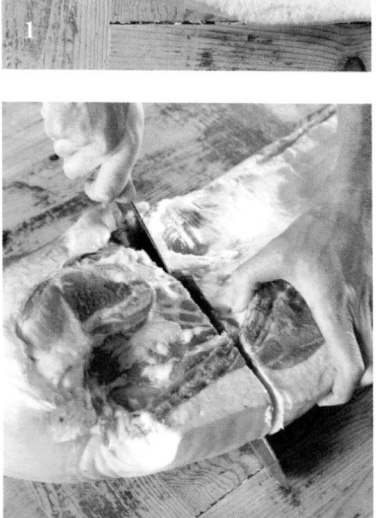

The loin and belly

If you leave the loin and the belly as one cut, it is termed the 'middle'. This can be dry-cured to make middle bacon. It can also be boned and rolled, then slow-roasted – much like the classic Italian dish porchetta, although, traditionally, this is made with a whole boned pig. However, it is more usual to separate the loin from the belly and cook them independently.

To separate the loin and belly, make a score line where you intend to make your cut (pic 1). This will be shallow over the rib bones but deeper once you are past them. The exact location of this mark depends how wide you want your belly to be, or how much tail you want on the loin, but as a guide I would suggest it should be roughly 10cm below the length of loin bone. A butcher might cut his loins wider because they command a higher price per kilo than the belly. But you don't have to think about margins here, only about what you like.

The next part of this manoeuvre requires a dexterous hand. Lay the middle over your left lower arm, if you are right handed, so that it naturally bows at that point. This makes it much easier to use the saw effectively. Being extremely careful, follow your knife cut mark from top to bottom, with short strokes of the saw (pic 2). You will hear and feel each rib you cut through. Don't cut any deeper or you may injure yourself! Use the steak knife to finish the job with a nice clean cut (pic 3), separating the entire loin from the belly.

The divided carcass

This first butchery session, dividing the carcass into the primal cuts, shouldn't take long at all. In fact you could stop right there and use the cuts as follows:

- You can slow-roast the whole shoulder and feed 25 people.
- The whole leg could be salted and air-dried.
- You can make the entire belly into streaky bacon if you like.
- The loin can be cooked on the bone for a celebratory feast.

Generally, unless you are cooking for a crowd, it is more convenient to divide the primal cuts into smaller joints (see overleaf).

Dividing the loin and belly

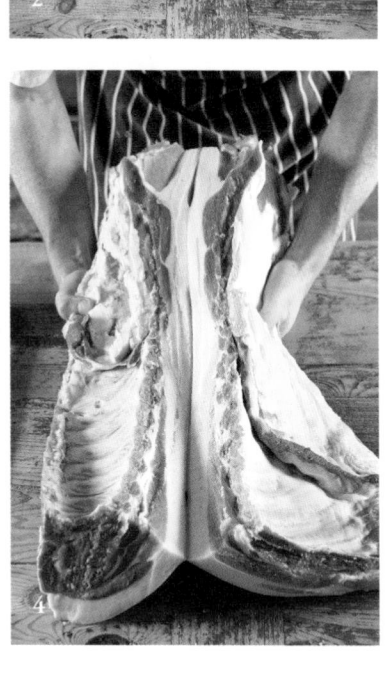

The secondary cuts

Each of the primal cuts can be divided further to give you a broader array of more manageable cuts. This is the point where you need to make decisions about what you really want from your pigs, what cuts you like best, how many people you intend to feed and even the recipes you might use the pork in. All these factors will influence how you butcher the primal cuts from here on. For example, if you're not a fan of chops but you love roast loin of pork, then you'll obviously cut several generous joints for your forthcoming Sunday lunches and forgo the chops.

Key

1 Boned and rolled spare rib
2 Diced hand
3 Hock
4 Skin
5 Boned and rolled loin
6 Back fat
7 Loin chops
8 Tenderloin
9 Belly joint (thick end)
10 Belly joint (middle cut)
11 Belly joint (tail end)
12 Diced tail end of belly
13 Flare fat
14 Whole chump
15 Leg steak
16 Whole boned leg
17 Trotter

Dividing the shoulder

The shoulder can be simply split into the whole spare rib and the hand and hock.

Make a score mark a few centimetres below the lowest part of the spinal bone from the front of the shoulder to the back, then use the saw to cut through the rib bones (pic 1). Stop and return to the boning knife (pic 2), gradually easing the knife down and across until you come to the ball and socket joint. Use the tip of your knife to sever the connection between the joints, then complete the cut with your larger steak knife (pic 3) to separate the spare rib from the hand and hock (pic 4).

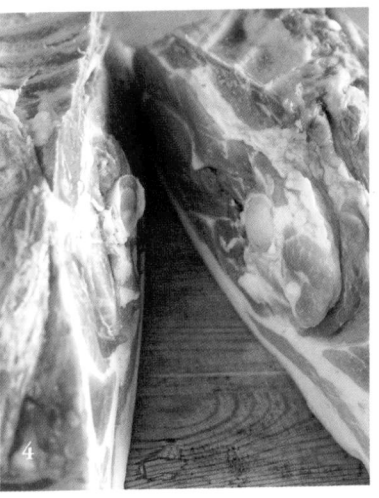

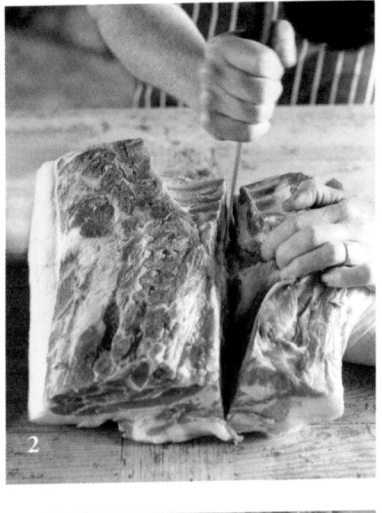

Splitting the hand and hock

I find it more useful to separate the hand from the hock for cooking purposes and it is pretty straightforward to do.

Insert your boning knife into the hock just below where it abuts the lower part of the shoulder termed the 'hand' (pic 1). Gradually cut around the circumference of the hock (pic 2). There is quite a specific joint in here and it can be difficult to negotiate. So once you've made your cut down to the bone, move to the saw and cut the hock free, then finish with the knife (pic 3) to separate the joints (pic 4).

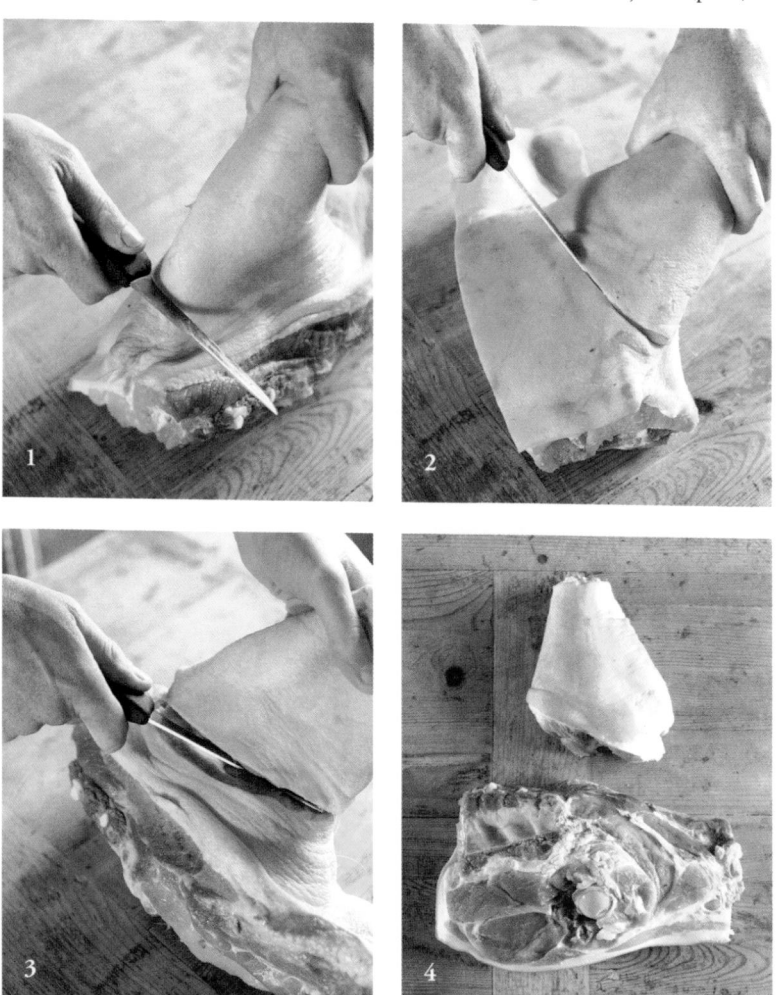

Boning the spare rib

The whole spare rib is a wonderful roasting joint and is quite easy to bone and roll.

Start by removing the section of spine, which carries below it the point of the ribs. Make your first cut under the ribs and tease them away from the meat with the knife tip (pic 1). When you reach the nodular underside of the front of the spine, remove it with the knife tip; try not to leave much meat on the bone (pic 2).

If you removed the shoulder at the right place, between ribs 4 and 5, then you should be able to see the tip of the blade bone clearly. This runs into the shoulder

and down to the socket joint that connects this cut to the hand. To remove this, locate the tip of the blade bone and cut around it. Trace it into the shoulder (pic 3); it will thicken out and turn down towards the socket joint. Work round the underside, which will have a distinct ridge, and over its top edge. It should come free fairly easily (pic 4).

Once the blade bone is removed, you're ready to roll and tie your whole spare rib joint. It can then be divided into two or even four smaller joints. If you plan to stuff the joint, now is the time to do so.

Using the shoulder for sausages If you plan to make lots of sausages you might like to mince the whole shoulder, but it's still wise to split the spare rib from the hand and hock, as it makes it more practical to remove the skin and bones. Follow the above instructions for preparing the spare rib, but instead of tying the joint, remove the skin and cube the meat. It's important to get your fat to lean balance correct. I like about 25% fat but, as it is only ever worked out by eye, this is a rough guide.

Scoring the skin for crackling

Scoring pig skin can be difficult with a regular knife. It's tough stuff, so a sharp Stanley knife is very useful. You can also set the blade's depth, which means you won't cut down through the fat into the flesh.

Start by setting the depth of the blade. Hold it against the fat and adjust the blade so you won't cut through into the meat. Carefully score the top and bottom edges of the joint (pic 1), then score nice straight lines through the middle section (pic 2). Try to keep your spacing as equal as possible; 2cm intervals are fine.

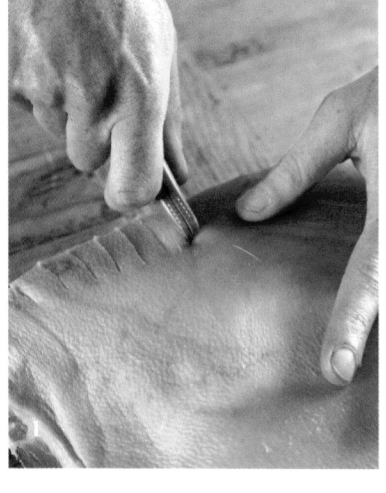

The butcher's knot

Like most knots, this takes a little time to master, but it is invaluable for tying boned and rolled joints. I'm illustrating it here to secure a boned-out spare rib joint.

Place your joint in front of you. Make your first knot in the middle of the joint and your second and third at either end. Then you can fill in the gaps as required.

Take your roll of butcher's string and run it under the joint (pic 1), giving you enough free string either side to make and secure your knot; cut the string. Tie a simple overhand knot at the end of the string furthest from you (pics 2 and 3).

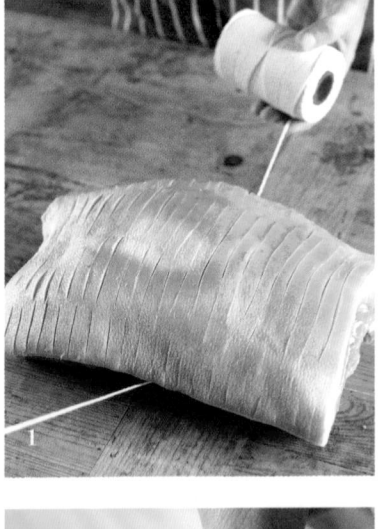

Lift up the end of the string nearest to you, then bring the knotted end around the back (pic 4) and secure it to the taut piece of string using a half hitch (pic 5). This will run up and down on itself like a slip knot.

Take the string you've been holding and firmly pull it upwards and towards you (pic 6). The slip knot will pull down on itself and become really tight. To finish, lock off the knot by looping the free end down at the base then, reaching through with your thumb and forefinger (pic 7), pinch the short tail of string and slip the loop down over it (pic 8), then pull tight and this will stop it coming undone.

There are several main joints that may need tying, including the boned loin, boned spare rib, the leg or half leg and sometimes the chump. Tying the prepared joints, particularly those that have been boned out, helps the joint keep its shape while it is being cooked.

You can divide the secured joint in half or into three or four smaller joints, depending on the cut, but you will have to make sure you have sufficient strings in place to hold them all together neatly, particularly if the joint has been stuffed.

Dividing the pork belly

You will need to decide how you want to use your pork bellies before you embark on cutting them up. I like to make some into bacon and keep some fresh for slow-roasting as joints.

A whole pork belly can be cut into several joints. The front of the belly (the end closest to the head) is called the 'thick end'. This first section, where the ribs are at their widest, is a prime roasting joint with the perfect balance of fat to meat.

The other end, sometimes called the 'tail end', is inclined to be a bit fattier and not as evenly layered with lean. I most often use this end for pâtés and sausages. If you intend to make bacon from your bellies they can be left whole or cut into two or three pieces.

Removing the flare fat Any pig that's carrying a good layer of back fat will also carry a nice sheet of flare fat. This can be found below the kidney and running over the best part of the pork belly itself. It's also called leaf fat and, once rendered, produces the best lard. This is perfect to use for roasting your potatoes, or making flaky pastry.

I remove this flare fat before cutting the pork belly, by simply peeling it off (pic 1). It will come away easily and often in a single piece.

I render the flare fat in a very low oven or in a pan set over a very low heat. Alternatively it can be frozen until needed.

Dividing the belly You will get three or four 1kg roasting joints from the belly with some trim from the tail end.

To portion the belly into three pieces, mark two cuts over the face of the belly from top to bottom, to give roughly equal-sized pieces. Use the saw to cut through the ribs (pic 2) and finish off with the knife (pic 3).

I usually leave the bone in when I roast the belly, but if I plan to cook ribs (see p.199) at any point, I will remove them. It's possible to freeze the ribs until you have enough to do a big dish of them for lots of friends.

Removing the ribs To remove the ribs, make a cut at the top corner of the thick end immediately under the ribs. Keeping the flat of the knife tight to the underside of the belly bones, work carefully and slowly down from the corner (pic 4), gradually separating the ribs. Eventually you'll come to two or three lengths of cartilage or softer bone, running the length of the belly. Cut under this cartilage and remove it, along with the ribs.

Dividing the loin

The loin can be cut into chops, cured for back bacon, or roasted. The chump is situated at the rear end. The tenderloin sits in its own pocket underneath the chump.

Removing the tenderloin Locate the tenderloin (pic 1). Starting at its top edge where the face of the spine runs, use the tip of the boning knife to encourage the tenderloin to come away (pic 2). It's only connected by membrane, so a combination of pulling and easing with your knife (pic 3) will enable you to release it (pic 4).

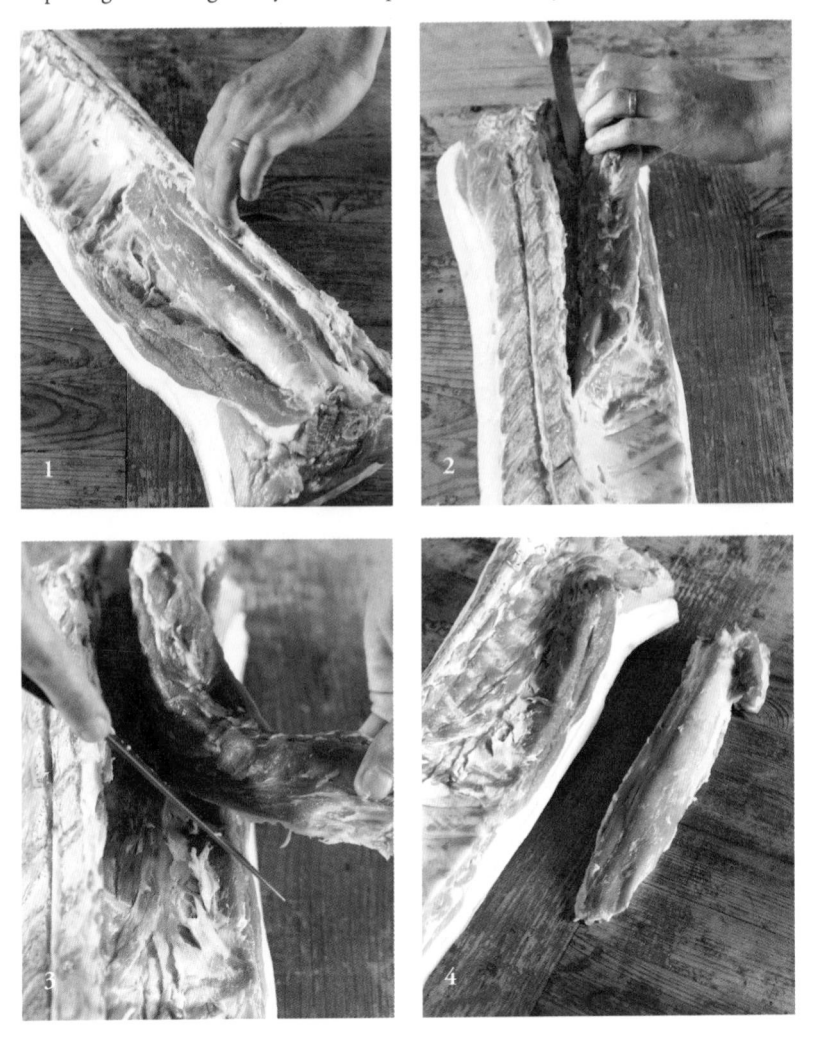

Removing the chump A fine, well-marbled joint in its own right, the chump can be easily removed from the long loin and cooked separately. Note where the spine turns down and the nature of the bone changes, about 12–15cm in from the end (pic 1). With your boning knife, make a cut down through to the bone (pic 2).

The chump can be boned out quite easily. Trace the tip of the knife around the bone that runs down to the spine (pic 3); it is quite deep in places. Carry the knife round and under the flat of the spine bone to work it free (pic 4). A whole chump, boned and rolled, would feed 4; alternatively it can be cut into chump chops.

Chining the loin The loin can be divided into two large, or three or four smaller, roasting joints. It's a top roasting joint and probably commands the highest price per kilo of all the prime cuts. Pork loin can be cooked on or off the bone. If roasted on the bone, which some people say gives you the best flavour, you will need to remove the bone before carving.

Along the length of the loin you will find the chine bone; this is the lower part of the spine. If you intend to cut chops or make back bacon, the chine bone needs to be removed first. If you are roasting your loin on the bone, it isn't essential to remove the chine bone first, but you may prefer to do so, to make carving easier. For this task, you will need to use your butcher's saw. Make sure it is sharp or this can be quite a challenge.

Place the loin skin side down on the surface. Take hold of the saw and start your cut at one end (pic 1), working consistently back towards the other. I use the groove in which the spinal cord sat as a guide. Follow this groove from one end to the other to free the chine bone (pic 2). Save it for making stock.

Portioning and boning the loin You can now cut your loin into suitably sized joints or chops. Simply mark portion cuts with your boning knife along the length of the loin, then cut through the bone with the saw (pic 1).

To bone the loin, run your boning knife down the inside edge of the top of the ribs (pic 2). Keep the flat of your knife as close to the bones as possible and don't let it stray. The trick is not to rush this – you don't want to leave lots of meat on the bone. You'll need to negotiate the point where the bones turn and flatten out. It will involve you carefully working the knife at an angle but always keeping the flat edge pressed to the bone.

Some rare-breed pigs carry more fat than others, particularly along the top of the loins. This back fat is a valuable commodity in the kitchen. If you think there is an excessive amount of fat on your pork loin and it would be better used for another purpose, you can remove it and tie the skin back on afterwards.

Skinning the loin The great thing about tying the skin back on is the flexibility it offers during cooking. If your pork is ready but your crackling is not, the crackling can be removed easily and popped back into a hot oven to finish off. Or, if the crackling is cooked and the pork is not, you can remove the crackling and return the pork to the oven. This technique can be applied to a variety of other cuts, too.

It's important to remove the skin in one piece, otherwise it can be difficult to tie back on to the joint. Once you've removed the sheet of skin and underlying fat you can trim back the fat, ideally keeping it in as few pieces as possible. You will be left with a leaner loin, leaner skin and some lovely fat that you can use for something else. This fat is ideal for making salami and pâtés.

Start by removing the skin and fat. Make a long sweeping cut with the boning knife along the edge of the length of the loin just above where the fat tops the meat, keeping a check on the depth to ensure you don't cut into the meat or the skin. Make a further gradual series of long shallow cuts (pic 1) to remove the skin and fat in one piece. Trim the fat on the skin to the required thickness (pic 2). Now score the skin as shown on p.101. Reposition the skin on top of the loin (pic 3). Use the butcher's knot (pp.102–3) to secure the skin back around the loin (pic 4).

The joint can now be refrigerated or frozen or cooked straight away.

Cutting chops To cut pork chops, stand the loin on the board. Make cuts down between the rib bones neatly and evenly until you come to the very base (pic 1). Use the cleaver or saw to cut through the bone and separate the individual chops (pic 2).

If your pork is carrying a lot of fat you may want to trim the chops, saving this trimmed back fat to use in other ways. Use the tip of the knife to trim away the skin and as much fat as you see fit (pic 3). You could use the trimmings to make my pork scratchings (p.206). Your chops are now ready for cooking (pic 4).

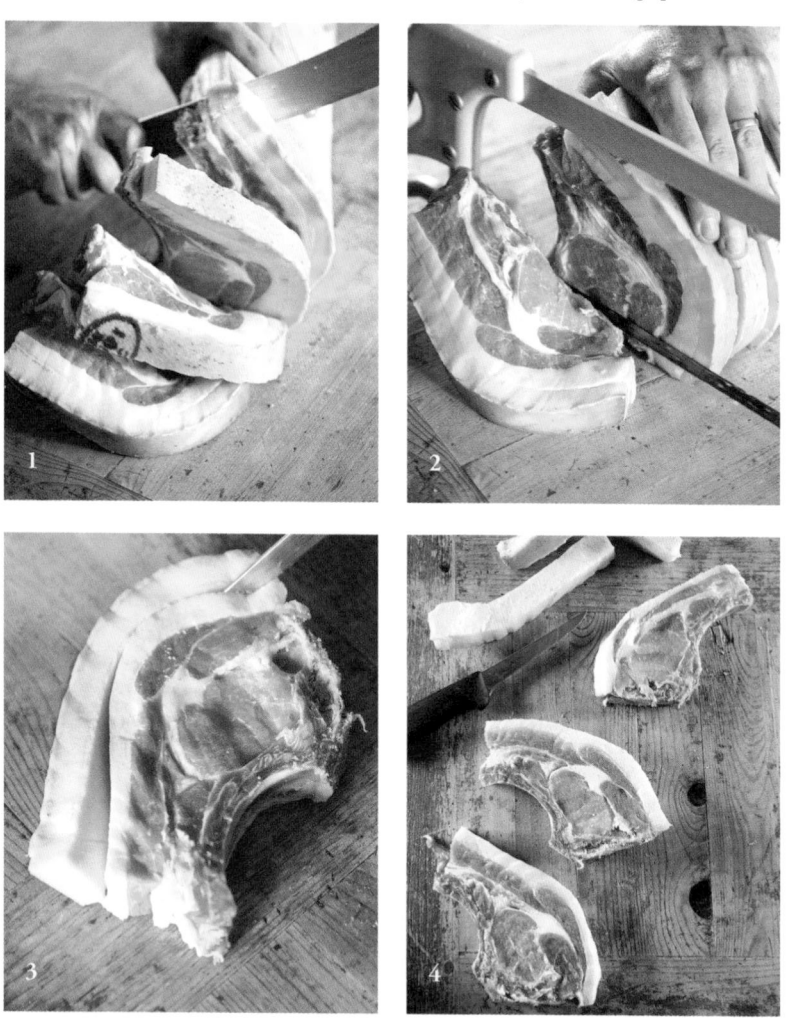

Dividing the leg

You should consider in advance how you want to use the leg, as it can be prepared in a number of different ways. If you intend to cure and air-dry a leg of pork for a classic prosciutto-style ham, you won't need to carry out much preparation at all. The leg can be effectively cured whole in the traditional way with the trotter still on and the bone still in.

Alternatively, the whole leg can be boned and rolled if you intend to make a wet-brined gammon or roast a whole leg of pork. The trotters can then be used in a separate recipe, as can the hock.

With a large leg of pork, it is possible to break it down into individual muscle sets in the same way a butcher would cut a leg of beef. You can achieve similar cuts, i.e. top side, rump, silverside, etc. The process is often termed seam butchery and could be considered advanced, but that doesn't mean you can't have a go.

Removing the aitch bone When I cure a leg of pork for an air-dried ham, I like to remove the aitch bone, which will expose the ball joint at the top of the leg. Removing this bone makes it easier to slice or even bone out the ham once it is dry, a year or so later.

You can see the flat face of the aitch bone at the top of the leg. You will have used it as a guide when you cut the leg from the middle.

Use the tip of the boning knife to cut around this bone (pic 1) until you get down to the ball and socket joint, which you will find on the underside of the aitch bone. Cut through the connective tissue to release the aitch bone (pic 2).

For instructions on how to cure a whole pork leg, see pp.235–6.

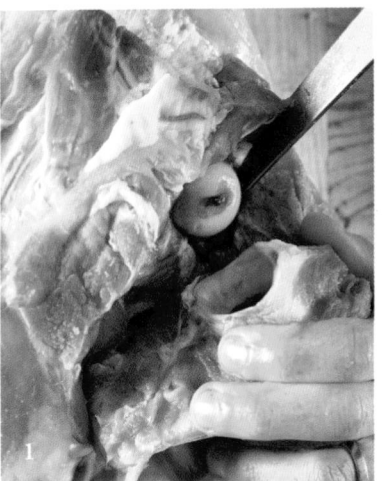
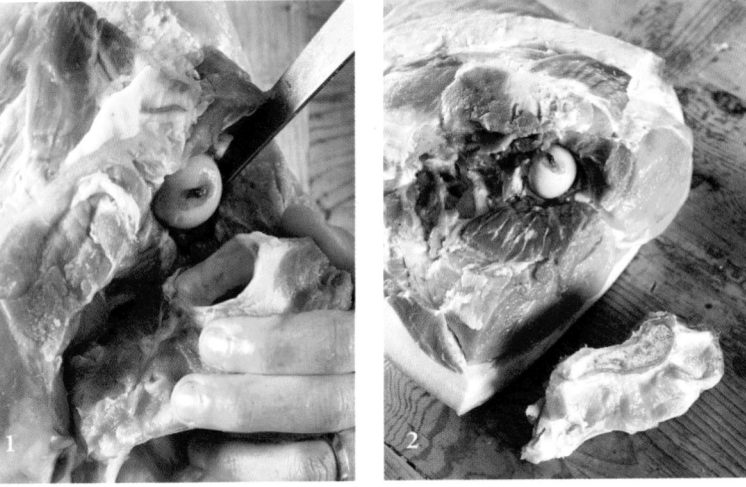

Removing the trotter The hock and trotter can be separated without the use of the saw. There is a specific point where you can divide the joint at the elbow.

Run your finger down the front edge of the leg until you come to a small indent, a gap in the bone where the tissue gives slightly, about halfway down. Insert the tip of the knife (pic 1); it should move easily into the joint – if it doesn't, you might need to be a bit higher. Grip the knife firmly and work it down through the joint, using a twisting motion (pic 2). You're looking to cut through a main tendon (pic 3) and when it's severed, you'll feel it release, separating the hock and trotter (pic 4).

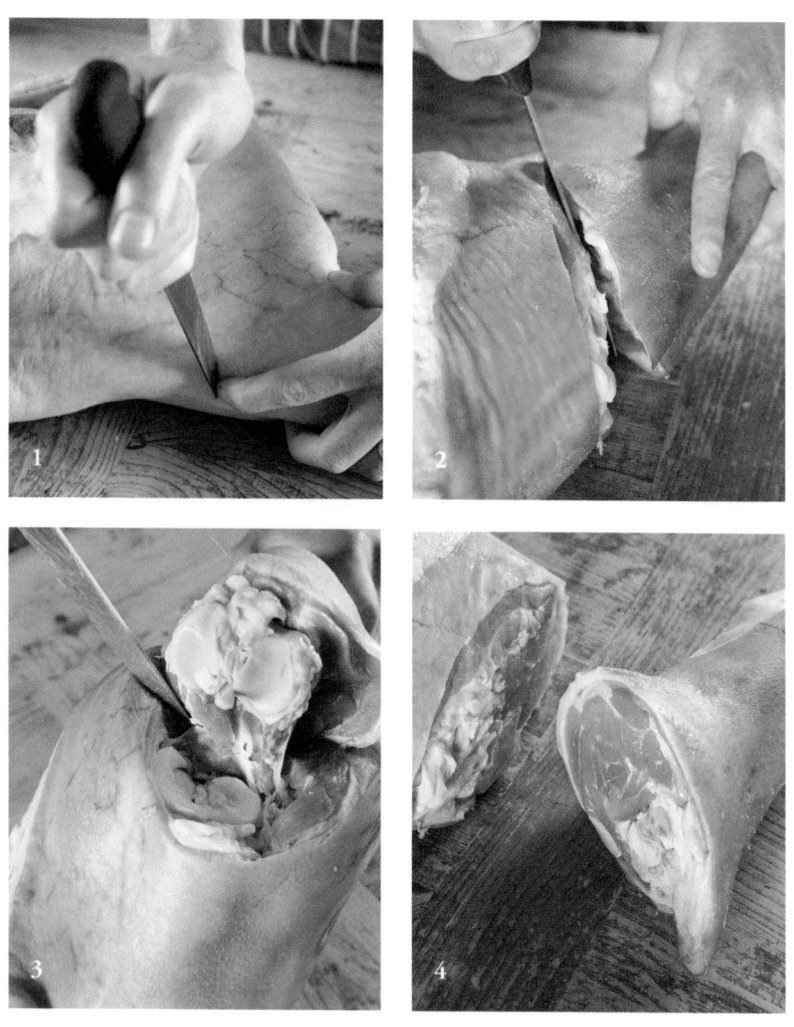

Boning the trotter

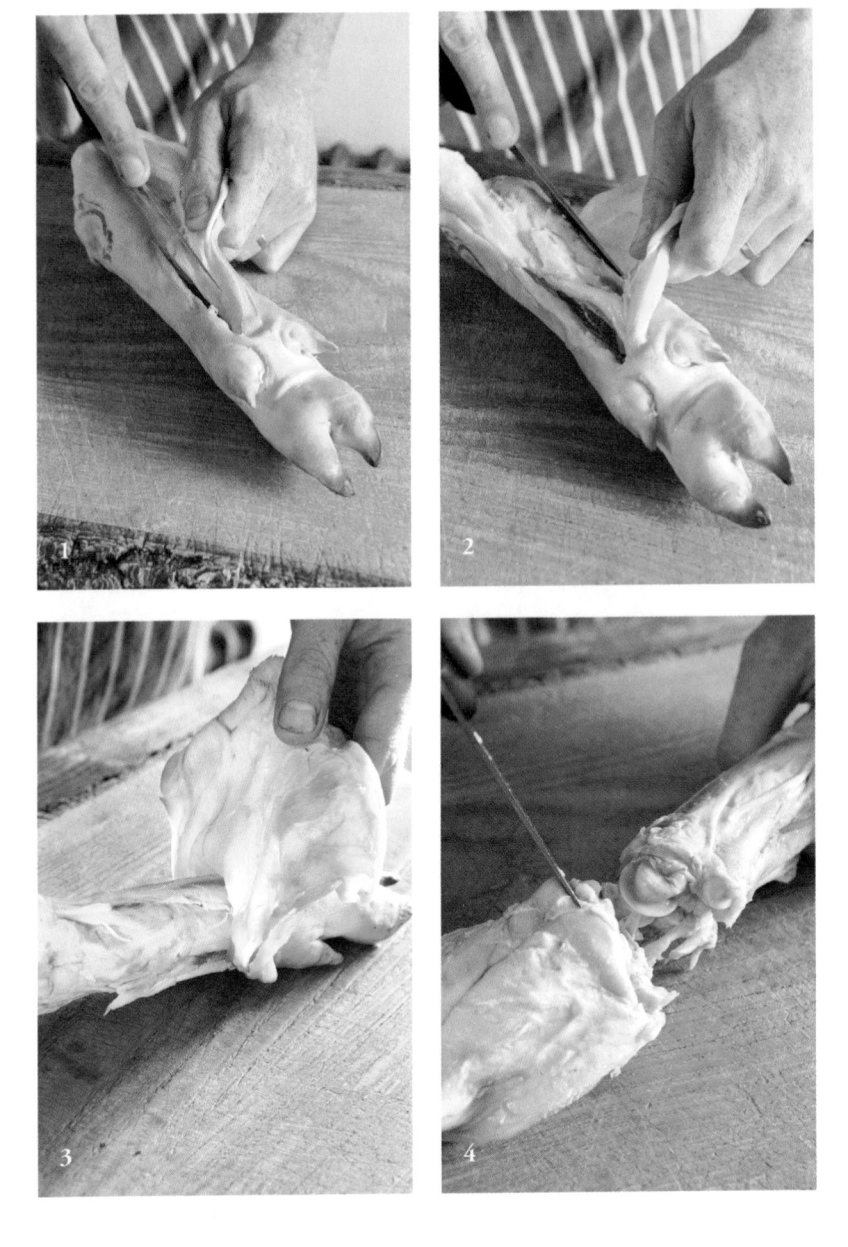

Boning the trotter There is nothing difficult about removing the bone from the trotter. In fact, it is a particularly satisfying process to carry out, and once complete opens up a variety of gastronomic opportunities, including my recipe for stuffed pig's trotters on p.187.

The secret is to use a sharp, sturdy boning knife and to take your time. Ideally, you want to avoid tearing the skin, so a slow and steady approach will ultimately pay off.

You'll see the exposed tendon on the back of the pig's trotter. Make your first cut by following this incision up to the top of the trotter (pic 1) with your boning knife. Now, using the tip of that very sharp knife, start teasing the skin away from the bone. You need to carefully cut right down to the centre of the ankle joint, working your way around the entire circumference of the trotter (pic 2). Ease the skin down to its lowest point (pic 3), using the tip of the knife to free any areas as you go.

Some force and precision will be needed to cut down through the tendons that form part of the ankle joint, to release the bone (pic 4). The boned trotter is ready for cooking.

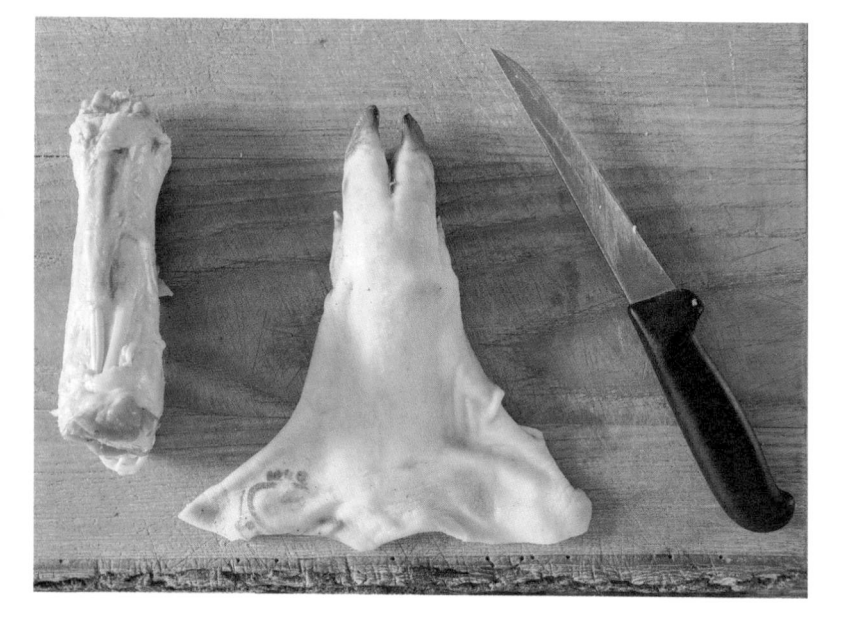

Boning the leg

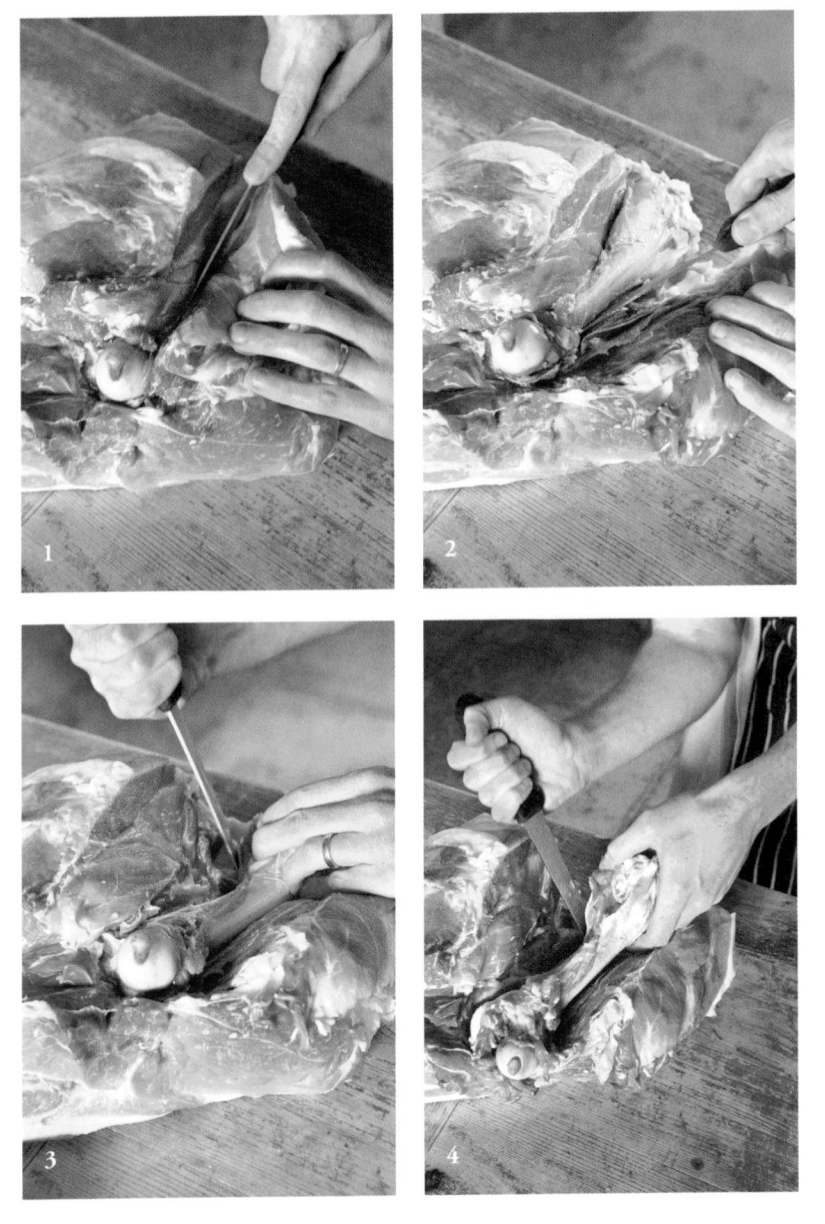

Boning the whole leg First remove the trotter (see p.113), then remove the aitch bone from the top of the leg (as described and shown on p.112). Once those two stages are complete, you can turn your attention to removing the main leg bone.

Place the tip of the knife on the exposed ball joint, then run it down the leg along the length of the bone (pic 1) until you get to the base, the chunky knuckle (pic 2). Use the knife to slowly cut down either side of the bone, gradually exposing more and more of the bone as you go (pic 3).

Work the knife underneath the bone and around the larger top and bottom sections until it comes free (pic 4). Occasionally the kneecap will be left in place; if so it needs to be removed. It lies at the base of the leg where the two joints were separated and, as you would expect, it is knee cap-shaped. Simply cut through any connective tissue and remove.

The boned leg is now ready to be rolled and roasted fresh for Sunday lunch or traditionally brined; see my Christmas ham recipe on p.229. You can cut nice leg steaks from it at this stage or cube it up for a big stew or curry, such as the pork and pumpkin curry on p.182.

The head

The pig's head offers some wonderful gastronomic possibilities. What's more, it accounts for more than 10% of the total weight of the animal so, if you've reared your own, it would be madness not to use it. (If you don't keep pigs, you can order a free-range or organic pig's head from your butcher.) The following instructions for preparing the head for cooking will enable you to get the best possible results. It's easy to feel overwhelmed by the thought of tackling this part of the pig, but it's not hard to familiarise yourself with it.

Place the pig's head on a board or your cutting table, face up. Use your sharp boning knife to cut the ears off at their base, where they meet the head (pic 1, overleaf). It's important that you reveal the ear canals so they can be cleaned. Make a cut at the base of each ear so you can open them up (pic 2) and give them a good clean. I use a stiff vegetable brush or a clean metal scourer for this job.

Remove the eyes one at a time (if they are still in place). Run the tip of the knife around the inside of the eye socket. Once you've released the eye, cut the connective tissue behind it and remove it completely. The eyes can be discarded.

Make a clear and defined score line from the top of the head down to the snout. Flip the head over so it is facing away from you. Take the saw and cut the head in half as equally as you can (pic 3). Once it is split (pic 4), you must remove the brain. I do this using a teaspoon (pic 5). It will be in two halves, and should come out easily. The brain can be refrigerated straight away.

It is now essential to remove any hairs and bristles from the head and ears. (Note that you must do this with the trotters and tail as well if you're planning to use them in a brawn.) Either singe off the hairs by holding the head, and then the ears, over a gas hob (pic 6), or use a cook's blowtorch if you prefer. Now use a knife to scrape away the burnt stubble (pic 7). Any stubborn, coarse areas can be cut away. Be really thorough at this stage because it will make a difference when you come to use the head, or any part of it, in a recipe. Finding black hairs in a slice of brawn is not at all nice.

Once you've singed the head, it needs a good clean. Hold it under cold running water (pic 8) and scrub it thoroughly all over. Repeat this process with the ears.

Now soak the pig's head overnight in a light brine made with four parts water to one part salt. This helps to clean the head, draws out any excess blood and has a light pickling effect, which will not only season the meat but change its texture a little too. The head is now ready for cooking. Try my brawn recipe on p.178 or my crispy pig's ears on p.158.

Preparing the head

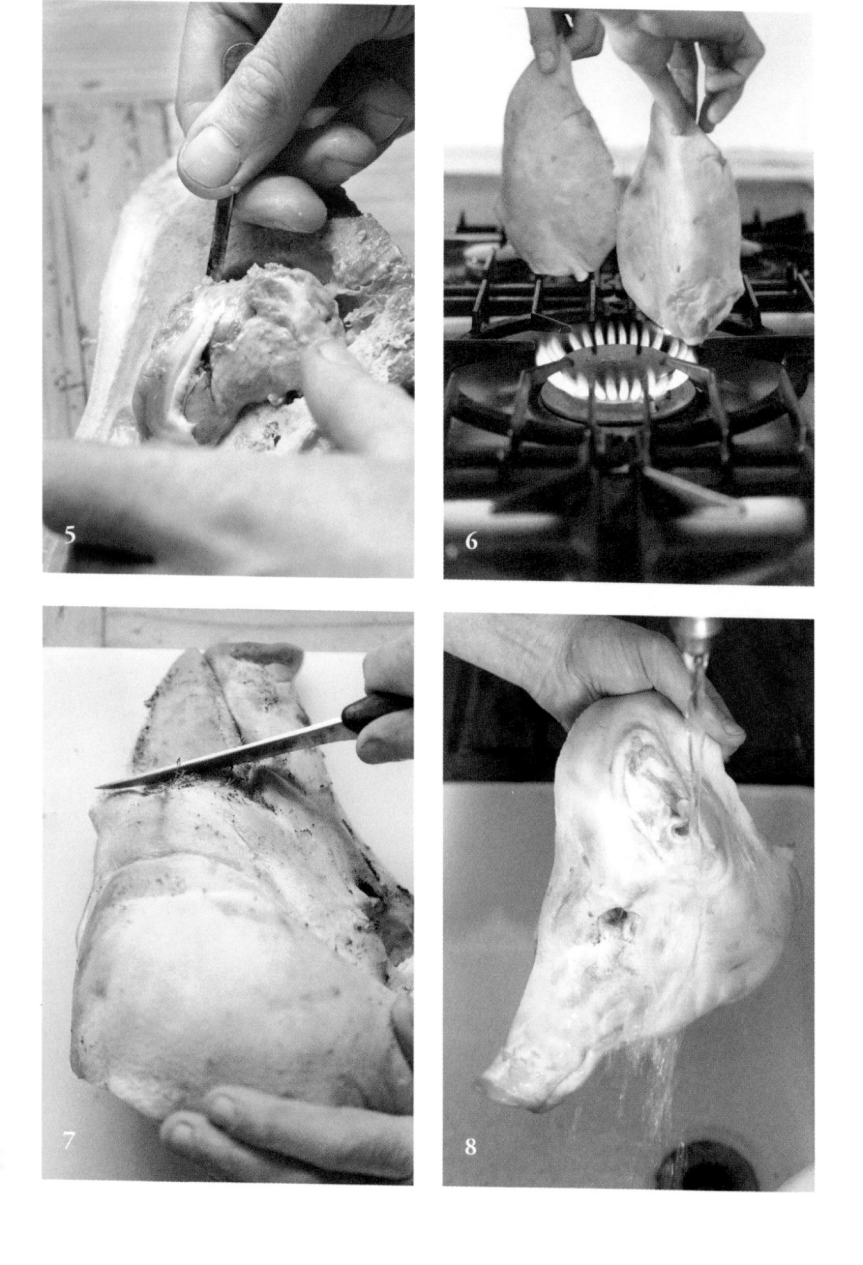

Cuts and recipes

The following chart lists the various cuts and offal you will get from a pig and delicious dishes you can turn them into, using recipes that I've included in the book. You'll find it helpful as a quick reference guide when you come to make decisions about what to cook and how.

CUT	RECIPE	PAGE
Head	Brawn	p.178
Cheeks	Pressed pig's cheek terrine	p.225
	Pig's cheeks and snail salad	p.147
Tongue	Tongue with salsa verde and lentils	p.176
Ears	Crispy pig's ears with fennel and lemon mayonnaise	p.158
Brains	Brains with sage and caper butter	p.154
	Brain McNuggets	p.160
Shoulder	Pulled pork	p.201
	Breakfast sausages	p.133
	Toulouse sausages	p.135
	Sage and onion sausages	p.136
	Big sausage rolls	p.216
	Pork pie	p.211
	Saucisson sec	p.219
	Chorizo	p.221
	Pork, sage and apple burgers	p.143
Loin	Pork chops with anchovies, rosemary, garlic and chilli	p.148
	Pork and piccalilli sandwich	p.205
	Roast pork loin with black pudding and beetroot	p.193
Tenderloin	Tenderloin with courgettes, dill, mint and spring onions	p.167
	Tenderloin with peaches, honey and almonds	p.169
Chump	Barbecued pork chump with herbs	p.164
	Chump chops with scallops and celeriac mash	p.144

CUT	RECIPE	PAGE
Pork belly	Bacon with beans and squid	p.185
	Home-cured streaky bacon	p.222
	Simple roast pork belly with fennel and coriander seeds	p.196
	Pork rillettes	p.238
	Rillons	p.243
	Slow-roast pork belly with chargrilled asparagus and mint	p.202
Leg	A Christmas ham	p.229
	River Cottage prosciutto	p.235
	Pork and pumpkin curry	p.182
	Pork with leeks and pancetta in cider and cream	p.181
Trotters	Terrine of pig's trotters and ham hock	p.175
	Stuffed pig's trotters with ceps, bacon and potato	p.187
Tail	Brawn	p.178
	Pig's tail and damsons	p.190
Liver	Liver and bacon	p.151
	Pâté de campagne	p.208
	Faggots	p.140
Spleen	Pig's spleen with red wine, marjoram and onions	p.189
Heart	Faggots	p.140
Lungs	Faggots	p.140
Blood	Black pudding	p.137
	Black pudding Scotch eggs	p.157
	Chocolate truffles with pig's blood and fennel	p.245
Kidneys	Devilled kidneys	p.152
	Chargrilled kidney wraps with North African flatbreads	p.161
Bones	Pork stock	p.171
	Sticky ribs	p.199
Skin	My pork scratchings	p.206
Fat	Smalec	p.240

Recipes

Sausages

I can't think of any other product that varies so much in quality as the humble sausage. At one end of the spectrum, there are excellent artisan sausages made using only the finest cuts of free-range and organic pork and a considered choice of seasonings. At the other end are highly processed economy-grade sausages made from mechanically retrieved or slurry meat, emulsified with a cocktail of colourings, preservatives, flavour enhancers and other additives. The cheapest may contain as little as 32% meat, invariably from factory-farmed pigs, and this so-called 'meat' can be made up of more than 50% connective tissue, fat and skin.

If you plan to keep a few pigs at home, it's more than likely you'll be up for making your own proper sausages too. It's great fun, very easy and they will be, without doubt, the best sausages you've ever eaten. As with everything, practice makes perfect, but to begin with you just want to get in there and have a go. You'll find you get to grips with it pretty quickly, and when it comes to linking the sausages, any prior experience of making balloon animals will definitely pay off. Once you've mastered the process, the world of sausage-making is yours.

Here are a few important pointers before you get started:
- Kitwise, you'll be able to source all of the items you need online.
- You're also going to need some sausage skins, which are, again, easy to get hold of from specialist suppliers. I use natural sausage casings, which are the cleaned intestines of pigs and sheep (see p.128).
- Remember that all good sausages contain some fat – it lends flavour and keeps them moist. The best sausages are made using meat from the shoulder and belly. These cuts have an inherent fat content, which makes them perfect for the job.
- The mincing process generates heat, so the pork must be well chilled before you start. Refrigerate or put into the freezer for an hour or so before mincing.
- You must ensure your mincer is scrupulously clean, so wash the barrel, blade and plate with hot soapy water before use. I chill the barrel before using it as well. It helps to keep everything nice and cold.
- Play around with the flavourings, the texture and the salt level until you find a combination that works for you. I like to include some fresh herbs, such as sage, thyme and parsley, I use white and black pepper and, occasionally, I like my sausages ever so slightly garlicky. However, keeping things simple generally pays off, especially if you've reared your own pigs. You'll want to be able to taste the meat for what it is, not just the herbs and spices you choose to complement it with.

- The sausage recipes that follow give you weights for prepared meat, i.e. meat that has been skinned, boned and trimmed ready for mincing.
- After you've minced and mixed your sausage filling, always taste the mix and adjust the seasoning if required. To do this, heat a little oil in a frying pan, make a burger-sized patty from the mixture and fry it for 4–5 minutes on each side or until cooked through. Remember that the flavours will develop over time, so don't be tempted to add too much more in the way of spice – you're really just checking the saltiness of the mixture.
- You don't have to keep your own pigs to make your own fantastic sausages, just find a supply of good pork. Make 5–10kg batches and freeze them by the dozen. It will certainly be the cheapest way to get the very best sausages.

Mincing meat

You will need to bone and skin your meat in advance (see pp.98–101). For most domestic mincers, the meat needs to be cut up into fairly small cubes, otherwise it may struggle or jam: 2–3cm pieces should work well. Get to know your mincer and how it works. It must be assembled correctly and the blade kept nice and sharp.

Keep a close eye on your meat as it comes out through the plate of the mincer. The blade 'cuts' the meat just like a knife, which gives the sausage the correct texture. If it looks 'chewed', stringy or pasty, it needs adjusting.

Domestic mincer

Sausage skins

Pig's intestines, known as 'hog casings', are used for traditional-sized butcher's bangers, whereas narrower sheep's intestines, known as 'sheep's runners', give you chipolatas. For large sausages and salamis, beef intestines are used. Natural sausage skins come salted, in bundles of four or five lengths, each length being several metres long. They are preserved, so they keep well.

Natural sausage skins need to be soaked for 2–3 hours in fresh water before you use them. It's easy to get into a tangle with them, so try to find the ends of each length and leave them dangling over the edge of the bowl.

I always use natural casings, but artificial skins are available, extruded from collagen, a naturally occurring protein. They're nothing like the real thing, and have a synthetic look, feel and taste.

Filling sausages

It is important to keep your working area clean and dry, and have some kitchen paper on hand to wipe down surfaces as and when necessary.

Fit the correct-sized nozzle on to your sausage stuffer, then fill with your mixture. Crank the handle slowly: this will force the sausagemeat down through the chamber as far as the nozzle, expelling any air in the process. Now you can

Salted sheep's runners

Threading skins on to the nozzle

slide on your casings. Find one end and slip it over the nozzle then feed the entire length on. I find keeping the skins wet helps them go on easily.

With one hand on the skins to regulate their flow and one on the handle of the machine, turn out the sausages in a steady and confident manner. Make sure you don't overfill them or they may burst when you come to twist them off, or link them. Repeat the process with the remaining mixture.

Linking sausages

We've all seen the fumbling novice baffled by the process of linking sausages. It was once a familiar forfeit on family game shows. It can appear confusing but it's surprising how many pick it up first time, if shown the right way to go about it. Once you understand the process, you'll be linking sausages in your sleep, but if you are flummoxed by the technique, you can simply twist your sausages into the required lengths, place on a tray in the fridge and cut them when ready to cook.

Step-by-step guide to linking sausages:

- First you need to fill your sausagemeat into your chosen skins. Run the length of sausage through your hands. The idea is to even out the thickness of the sausage as it passes through your fingers. This is important because you don't want sausages that are really thick in one area and thin in another.
- Choose an end to start with and secure with a twist. Decide on the length you want your sausages to be and make your first pinch at this length. Twist firmly (pic 1 overleaf), giving it several turns of the wrist.
- Make a further two twists at similar equal intervals. You will now have three twisted, shaped sausages of the same size (pic 2).
- Take hold of the second pinched twist and lift the length of sausages up in front of you. Now turn the first twist round the third twist to form your first part link (pic 3).
- Now bring the tailing end of the sausage up to meet the top of your first two sausages (pic 4). Pinch it at the top, to create the third sausage in your link.
- Pass this sausage through the two held in your other hand to complete your link of three sausages (pic 5).
- Through the middle of this first link, pull through a length equal to two sausages from the free end (pic 6).
- Pinch this new section at its highest central point and again where it meets the link below (pic 7).
- Bring up another single sausage length from the tailing end to meet this top pinch (pic 8).
- You are now at the same stage as shown in pic 4, so from here follow the sequence from pic 5 onwards to link the remainder of your sausages.

Linking sausages

Storing sausages

Commercially produced sausages usually contain preservatives, which will extend their life – beyond a week in many cases. The fresh sausages that I have included recipes for here will keep well for 5 days in the fridge. I like to store them on a tray, lightly covered with a clean tea towel, or very lightly wrapped in greaseproof paper. This allows them to breathe, rather than sweat in a plastic bag.

Sausages freeze well. Bag them up in batches of 6, 12 or 24, according to how many you are likely to cook at any one time. It is preferable to do this once they have had a chance to dry in the fridge for a few hours, or if it's a dry winter's day, hang them outside in a cold wind. Defrost sausages thoroughly before cooking; I like to do this in the fridge overnight.

Cooking sausages

I think you get the best results by cooking sausages in a frying pan over a low heat. I add a dash of oil followed by the sausages and let them gently sizzle away, turning occasionally, until they are well browned and cooked through; this should take a good 20 minutes or more. Cooking them slowly actually helps to tenderise the pork inside and stops them splitting. You will also get a wonderful caramelisation. Don't be tempted to prick the sausages with a fork, as so often suggested – this just lets out all the fat and juices, which are far better kept inside.

Like a chop or a roast loin of pork, good sausages should be rested in the pan before you serve them. Just 5 minutes will give them a chance to relax, settle and cool slightly. If they're boiling hot inside you won't taste how good they really are. Grilling and oven cooking are good ways to cook sausages as well. If using the oven, preheat it to 190°C/Gas mark 5 and cook the sausages on a lightly oiled baking tray for 30–35 minutes, turning them once or twice. Grilling sausages makes quite a mess as they can spit and hiss a little under the fierce heat of the element. Keep a close eye on them and turn regularly so they cook evenly.

We love to throw a few sausages on the barbecue when the weather's fine and, when they're cooked well, they are superb. But the unpredictable nature of open-fire cooking means we've all been party to the odd carbonised catastrophe wedged within a floury finger roll.

Successful barbecue cooking is all about heat management. It's simple really. Allow your embers to lose their fierce edge before you put any food on to cook. Start your sausages on the outer part of the grill and get an idea of the heat and how quickly they are cooking before you move them closer in. If your barbecue has an adjustable grill, make use of it. Sausages should take 20–25 minutes, even on a barbecue.

Breakfast sausages

My children, who are my biggest critics, rave about these sausages. The mix is well flavoured with ground white pepper and freshly chopped thyme. It makes for a fine breakfast banger.

Makes 40–50 sausages

8 metres hog casings (see p.128)
2kg pork belly, well chilled
2kg pork shoulder, well chilled
400g dried breadcrumbs
40g salt
20g freshly ground white pepper
10g soft brown sugar

2 tbsp chopped thyme
200ml iced water

Equipment
Mincer
Sausage stuffer

Wash the salt off the casings or runners and leave them to soak for several hours in a bowl of fresh water, changing the water once or twice.

Cut the pork belly and shoulder into 2–3cm pieces. Keep a sharp eye out for any glands, membrane or gristle – you don't want to put these into your sausages.

Put the pork through the mincer fitted with the coarse plate (7–8mm). Catch the minced pork in a large mixing tray or bowl. Scatter over the breadcrumbs, salt, pepper, sugar and thyme. Mix thoroughly, then add the water and mix again. Put the entire mix through the mincer again, through the same-sized plate.

Fry off a small patty of the mix to check the seasoning (see p.127) and adjust the main mixture accordingly.

Chill the mixture while you wash your mincer and set up your sausage-stuffing machine. Keeping the mixture as cold as possible ensures it will go through the filler more easily; it also means your sausages will last longer.

Fill and link the sausages as described on pp.128–31. Store your sausages, well wrapped, in the fridge, where they will keep for 4–5 days. Alternatively, bag them up and freeze them.

Toulouse sausages

This great sausage is full of character. It is perfect grilled and served with olives and good bread, or gently braised with white beans and parsley. I use good red wine and smoked bacon, but you can use unsmoked (green) bacon, if you prefer.

Makes 60–70 sausages

10 metres sheep's runners (see p.128)
2.5kg pork shoulder, well chilled
A large glass of red wine
4 garlic cloves, peeled and grated
2 tbsp chopped thyme
10g freshly ground black pepper
200g dried breadcrumbs
30g salt

1kg clean white back fat, cubed, well chilled
500g raw smoked cubed ham or bacon, well chilled

Equipment
Mincer
Sausage stuffer

Wash the salt off the runners and leave them to soak for several hours in a bowl of fresh water, changing the water once or twice.

Cut the pork shoulder into 2–3cm cubes. Keep a sharp eye out for any glands, membrane or gristle – you don't want to put these in your sausages.

Mince the pork shoulder once using the coarse plate (7–8mm), catching the minced pork in a large mixing tray or bowl. Mix in the wine, garlic, thyme, black pepper, breadcrumbs and salt, then the cubes of fat and the ham or bacon. Put the mix back through the mincer. (Mincing the pork twice but the fat and bacon only once gives the mixture definition and, I find, improves the texture of this sausage.)

Fry off a small patty of the mix to check the seasoning (see p.127) and adjust the main mixture accordingly.

Chill the mixture while you wash your mincer and set up your sausage stuffer.

Fill and link the sausages as described on pp.128–31. Store your sausages, well wrapped, in the fridge, where they will keep for 4–5 days. Alternatively, bag them up and freeze them.

Sage and onion sausages

Deeply flavoured with caramelised onions and freshly chopped sage, these sausages are perfect for supper with good, honest buttery mash. I also like them in toad-in-the-hole – or in a bun with blue cheese and rocket leaves.

Makes 40–50 sausages

8 metres hog casings (see p.128)
2 tbsp lard
4 large onions, peeled and
    thinly sliced
3 tbsp chopped sage
2kg pork belly, well chilled
2kg pork shoulder, well chilled
400g dried breadcrumbs
15g freshly ground black pepper

10g coriander seeds, crushed
40g salt
10g soft brown sugar
200ml iced water
Sea salt and freshly ground pepper

Equipment
Mincer
Sausage stuffer

Wash the salt off the casings and leave them to soak for several hours in a bowl of fresh water, changing the water once or twice.

Place a large heavy-based pan over a medium heat. Add the lard and melt, then add the onions. Season with a little salt and pepper and give them a stir. Once they are frying well, turn the heat right down and pop a lid on the pan. Cook for 1 hour, stirring every 10 minutes. Don't let the onions burn; if you think they might, add a splash of water to the pan. Once they are caramelised, stir in the sage and take off the heat. Allow to cool, then refrigerate until you're ready to make the sausages.

Cut the pork belly and shoulder into 2–3cm cubes. Keep a sharp eye out for any glands, membrane or gristle, discarding any you find. Put the pork through the coarse plate of the mincer (7–8mm), catching the minced pork in a large mixing tray or bowl. Add the breadcrumbs, pepper, coriander, salt and sugar. Mince this mixture again then stir in the onions and water, giving everything a thorough mix.

Fry off a small patty of the mix to check the seasoning (see p.127) and adjust the main mixture accordingly.

Chill the mixture while you wash your mincer and set up your sausage stuffer.

Fill and link the sausages as described on pp.128–31. Store your sausages, well wrapped, in the fridge, where they will keep for 4–5 days. Alternatively, bag them up and freeze them.

Black pudding

Forget images of blood-splattered kitchens and complicated pagan-like processes. Making your own black pudding at home is easy and always feels exciting. It's hard to find black pudding made with fresh blood – the majority of puddings available in butchers' shops and supermarkets use dried blood, which gives you a drier pudding. If you're killing your own pigs, ask the abattoir to save you the blood. It freezes well, so you can easily make half the quantity I give below. Otherwise, it would be worth asking your local friendly butcher if he thinks he could source some fresh blood for you.

Makes 4 terrines or 12 sausage-style black puddings

1kg pork back fat, finely diced into 4–5mm cubes
1kg onions, peeled and finely diced
5g ground black pepper
5g ground mace
5g ground coriander
4g cayenne pepper
35g soft brown sugar
75g salt
250ml double cream
250ml brandy
2 litres fresh pig's blood

500g fine oatmeal
600g dried breadcrumbs
500g cooked pearl barley (125g uncooked weight)
About 6 metres beef middle casings (optional), soaked for several hours

Equipment
Sausage stuffer (if filling into skins)
4 x 1kg loaf tins (optional)
Cook's temperature probe (optional)

Place a large heavy-based pan over a low heat. Add a quarter of the fat and cook, stirring regularly, until it starts to render. Add the onions and cook until soft but not coloured, about 10–15 minutes. Add the rest of the fat to the pan along with all the ground spices, sugar and salt. Stir well.

Now remove the pan from the heat and pour in the cream and brandy, stirring. A few minutes later, once the pan has cooled a little, slowly add the blood, stirring all the time. Remove from the heat and fold in the oatmeal, breadcrumbs and cooked pearl barley.

Leave the mixture to stand for 30 minutes, to allow it to thicken as the cereals absorb the moisture. You then have two options: either baking the mixture in loaf tins or terrines (as described overleaf), or stuffing it into natural sausage casings in the traditional way and poaching (see overleaf); for this I use beef middle casings.

To cook the mixture 'blood cake' style, preheat the oven to 120°C/Gas mark ½ and line four 1kg loaf tins with cling film, leaving some overhanging the sides. Divide the mixture evenly between the tins and fold the overhanging cling film over the top. Cover each tin with foil, crimping it tightly around the edges. Set the tins in a roasting tray containing enough hot water to come two-thirds of the way up the sides. Cook in the oven for 1½ hours or until the internal temperature of the pudding, measured with a cook's temperature probe, registers 72°C. Allow the black pudding to cool before turning it out and refrigerating.

Alternatively, if you are filling the black pudding mixture into skins, do so in the same way as for saucisson sec (p.219). It's important not to overfill the casings as they can burst when you poach them. Use a very fine pin or needle to prick each pudding several times, particularly if you can see any air gaps. Bring a large pan of fresh water to the boil, then turn the heat down so it is barely simmering. Lower in the puddings, one at a time, and cook very gently for 35–40 minutes; do not allow to boil. Remove and allow to cool before refrigerating.

Once your black pudding is cooked, it can be eaten straight away, but it will keep in the fridge for up to 10 days; it also freezes successfully.

Black pudding can be eaten just as it, but generally people prefer to fry or grill it first. I like to slice it thickly and fry it for a few minutes on each side so it starts to crisp up ever so slightly. Traditionally, it is served with eggs and bacon. It's also delicious with any of the following: seared scallops, fried mackerel, roast chicken, roast pheasant, fried mushrooms, baked tomatoes, barbecued sweetcorn, buttered peas, sweet raw gooseberries and stewed rhubarb.

Faggots

Faggots are a traditional savoury, much loved throughout the Midlands and Wales, and something we make a lot at River Cottage. They are a good way to use the offal from a pig – minced, well-seasoned and wrapped in caul fat. They're delicious with smashed swede and onions.

Makes 18 faggots

500g pig's liver
1 pig's heart
500g pig's lights (lungs)
250g fatty pork belly
250g bacon pieces
1 onion, peeled and finely chopped
150g fresh breadcrumbs
A small glass of brandy
4 juniper berries, ground
3 garlic cloves, grated
A small bunch of thyme, leaves only, finely chopped

A small bunch of parsley, leaves only, chopped
A good grating of nutmeg
1½ tsp fine salt
½ tsp freshly ground black pepper
500g pork caul fat, soaked in warm water for 5–10 minutes
A trickle of oil, for frying

Equipment
Mincer

Trim out any tough ventricles from the liver. Do the same with the heart. Trim and cube the lights, then soak them in fresh water for 10 minutes. Skin, bone and cube the pork belly, then combine with the bacon, onion, liver, heart and lights. Pass the mixture through a mincer fitted with the medium plate (6mm). Transfer to a bowl, add all the other ingredients except the caul fat and mix well. Chill the mixture for 30 minutes.

Divide the chilled mixture into balls, each about the size of a small apple, and wrap each ball in a sheet of caul fat. Don't overwrap them – the caul just needs to encase the mixture. Refrigerate the faggots until you're ready to cook them.

Heat a heavy-based frying pan over a medium-high heat. Add a trickle of oil, followed by the faggots and reduce the heat to medium. Gently fry the faggots until golden brown on all sides and cooked through, 20–25 minutes should do it. Alternatively, they can be baked in the oven at 180°C/Gas mark 4 for 40 minutes, turning once or twice.

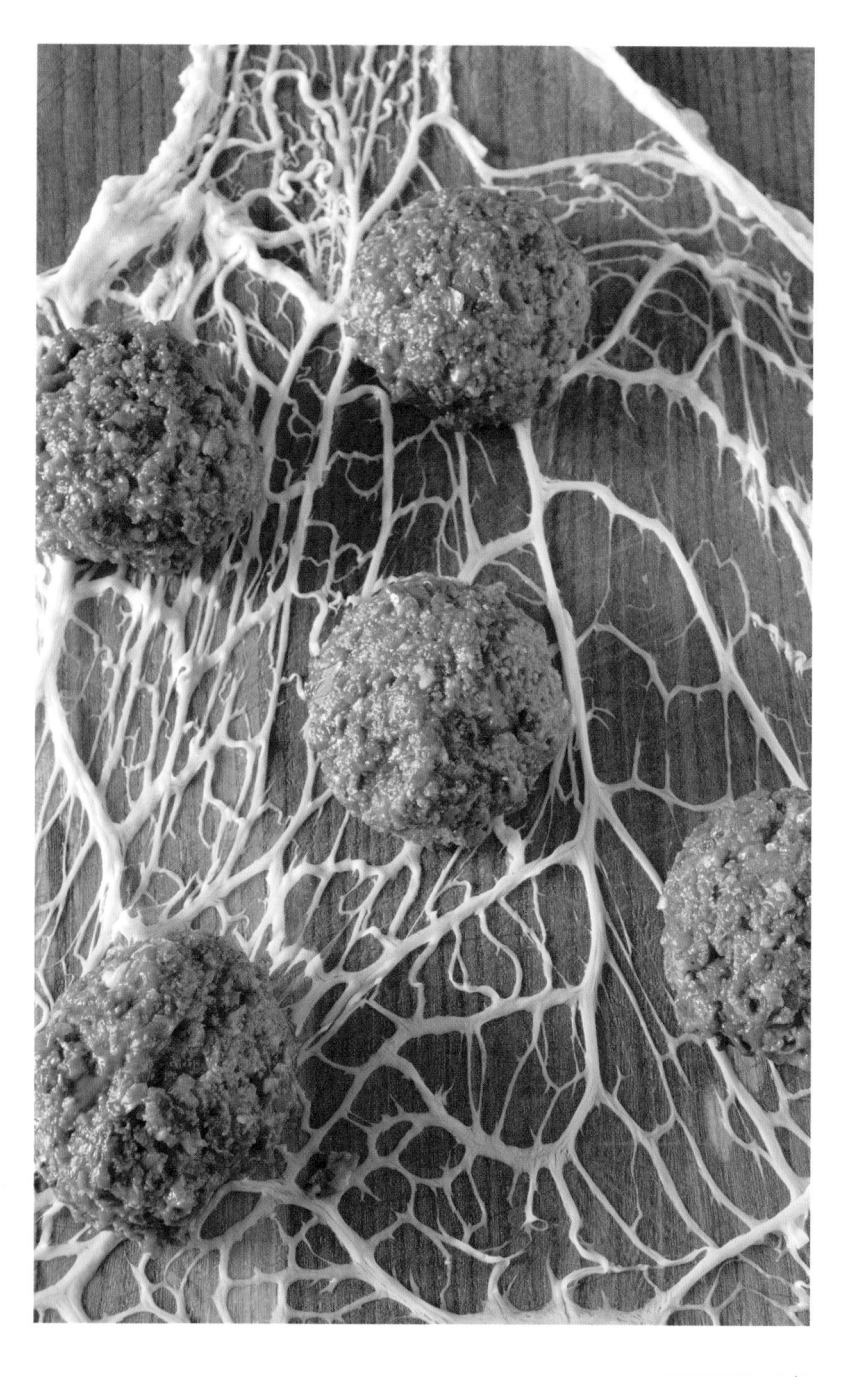

Pork, sage and apple burgers

Crushed coriander and lots of black pepper give these pork burgers a fruity tang you don't get from apple alone. Bold and big, they're perfect in a soft bap with good mustard. I like to keep the apple chunky so you know what's what when you come to eat them.

Makes 4–5 burgers

1 tsp coriander seeds
1 tsp black peppercorns
A handful of sage leaves
2 dessert apples
500g minced pork belly
50g fresh breadcrumbs
1 tsp salt

Finely grated zest of ½ lemon
A trickle of oil, or 1 tsp lard

To serve
Soft baps
Wholegrain mustard

Toast the coriander seeds and black peppercorns for 1–2 minutes in a dry pan until fragrant. Tip them into a mortar and bash with the pestle until well crushed.

Chop the sage leaves relatively finely. Peel, quarter and core the apples, then chop them into 3–4 mm cubes.

Combine the pork, breadcrumbs, crushed toasted spices, salt, lemon zest, chopped apple and sage in a bowl and mix thoroughly.

Shape the mixture into 4 or 5 large burgers, using your hands to mould them into a good, firm patty. Chill in the fridge for at least half an hour before cooking.

Heat a large frying pan over a medium heat. Add the oil or lard, followed by the burgers. Cook gently for 8–10 minutes or until just cooked through, turning the burgers halfway through.

Remove the pan from the heat and let the burgers rest for 5 minutes in the warmth of the pan. Serve in soft baps with a generous smear of wholegrain mustard.

Chump chops with scallops
and celeriac mash

This autumnal gem of a dish can be as rustic or as fancy as you like. It's a fine way to serve chops and can take centre stage at any supper party. Big earthy notes from the celeriac are balanced by the delicate sweetness of the scallops, while richness from the pork chops carries everything along.

Serves 4

A trickle of oil, or 1 tsp lard
4 chump chops, about 2–3cm thick, skinned
2 garlic cloves, bashed
8 hand-dived large scallops, cleaned
Sea salt and freshly ground black pepper

For the celeriac mash
1 celeriac, peeled and cubed
2 garlic cloves, peeled and sliced
2–3 sprigs of thyme
500ml pork stock (p.171), or chicken or veg stock
4 bay leaves
4 juniper berries, crushed
150ml double cream

For the celeriac mash, put the celeriac in a pan with the garlic, thyme, stock, bay leaves and crushed juniper. Bring to a gentle simmer, partially cover with the lid and cook until the celeriac is nice and tender, and the stock is well reduced; this will take 30–40 minutes. Drain, reserving the stock. Discard the thyme and bay.

Bash the celeriac with a potato masher to a coarse texture. Stir in the cream and heat through gently, stirring often, for 1–2 minutes. Season with salt and pepper to taste; keep warm.

Meanwhile, place a large frying pan over a medium-high heat and add the oil or lard. Season the chump chops all over and place them in the pan with the bashed garlic cloves (no need to peel them). Cook for 5–6 minutes on each side until golden and cooked through. Remove the chops to a warm plate to rest while you cook the scallops.

Discard the garlic and make sure the pan is good and hot. Season the scallops and place them in the pan. Cook for 1–2 minutes on each side, depending on size, but no longer or they will toughen.

To serve, spoon the celeriac on to warmed plates. Place the just-cooked scallops on top and a pork chop alongside.

Pig's cheek and snail salad

The combination of crispy pig's cheeks and tender snails has an earthy appeal to me. The addition of a little garlic, fresh parsley and sharp red wine vinegar turns them into a really special salad.

Serves 2

200g pig's cheek, including the skin
    and fat, poached and cooled
    (as for the recipe on p.225)
10–12 blanched, shelled Burgundy
    snails (available ready prepared)
2 garlic cloves, peeled and finely
    chopped
A small bunch of parsley, leaves only,
    chopped
A small bunch of chives, chopped
2 Little Gem lettuces, leaves separated

For the dressing
2 tbsp red wine vinegar
2 tbsp olive oil
1 tsp Dijon mustard
1 tsp sugar
Sea salt and freshly ground
    black pepper

Tear or cut the poached pig's cheek into 2–3cm pieces or shards. Place a large frying pan over a medium-high heat. Add the pig's cheek and fry until crispy and golden all over. Spoon or pour off the excess fat (save it for frying sausages).

Add the snails to the pan and fry for a further 2–3 minutes. Add the garlic and chopped parsley and chives, then season well with salt and pepper.

For the dressing, put all the ingredients into a jam jar, screw on the lid and shake thoroughly to combine.

Put the lettuce leaves in a large bowl and trickle over half the dressing. Arrange the dressed leaves over two plates and divide the warm pig's cheek and snails between them. Pour the rest of the dressing into a small jug to put on the table.

Serve the salad straight away, with some warm French bread and butter.

Pork chops with anchovies,
rosemary, garlic and chilli

It's good to pimp your pork chops once in a while, especially if you've got quite a few in the freezer. This is a simple and quick supper that all comes together in the one pan in less than 20 minutes. I use dried chilli in this recipe because I like the depth it brings, but you could use fresh, if you prefer.

Serves 4

A dash of olive oil
4 good-sized pork chops on the bone
8–10 anchovies
6 garlic cloves, peeled and sliced
2 dried chillies, deseeded and very
    thinly sliced

4 tender sprigs of rosemary
100ml water or cider
Sea salt and freshly ground
    black pepper

Place a large pan over a medium heat and add the oil. Season the pork chops all over with salt and pepper, then add them to the pan. Cook for 4–5 minutes on the first side, then flip them over and add the anchovies, garlic, chillies and rosemary, allowing the flavourings to fall in amongst and around the chops. Keep moving the contents of the pan around as you finish cooking the chops – they will need 4–5 minutes on their second side. Remove them to a warm plate to rest.

Toss the garlic and rosemary around the pan, then add the water or cider. Bring quickly to a simmer, with a shake and a stir, then let bubble until reduced down by half. Pour the reduced liquor over the chops and serve. This is good with roasted squash wedges.

Liver and bacon

My take on this timeless classic should convert even those who are most reluctant to eat liver. What's more, because the liver is served slightly pink, it all comes together quite quickly.

Serves 4

A trickle of oil
200g bacon lardons or streaky bacon, chopped
1 large onion, peeled and thinly sliced
2 garlic cloves, peeled and sliced
1 tbsp chopped sage
A splash of brandy (optional)

400ml pork stock (p.171) or chicken stock
2 sprigs of thyme
500g very fresh pig's liver
100g plain flour, for coating
An extra dash of oil, or 1 tsp lard
Sea salt and freshly ground black pepper

Heat a medium pan over a medium-low heat and add a small trickle of oil, followed by the bacon. Sauté until the pieces start to render a little fat and take on some colour. Add the onion and fry gently for 5 minutes, stirring as it cooks. Add the garlic and chopped sage and continue to cook for 3–4 minutes.

Now add the brandy, if using, and reduce by half. Pour in the stock, add the thyme and some pepper and bring to a simmer. Let simmer for 15–20 minutes, or until the liquid has reduced by two-thirds. Keep warm over a very low heat.

Meanwhile, trim any white ventricles from the liver, then carefully cut it into nice even slices, 1cm thick, using a sharp knife. Season the pieces of liver with salt and pepper, then dip them in the flour to coat.

Heat a large frying pan until hot, then add a little oil or lard. Now add the sliced liver and cook for 1 minute on each side, no longer. Remove the liver from the pan and add it to the bacon and onion mix. Toss the liver through and bring it all back to a simmer, but for no more than a minute.

Divide the liver, onion and bacon between warmed plates and serve with mash and mustard, or a summer salad.

Devilled kidneys

Originally a popular Victorian breakfast dish, devilled kidneys sometimes make an appearance in today's full-English fry-ups. It was Hugh who showed me how to make this particular version. I liked it so much that I've been cooking it ever since. It makes a lovely light lunch, or even a tasty starter. The sauce is particularly good.

Serves 2

4 very fresh pig's kidneys
1 tbsp lard or olive oil
A small glass of cider brandy
1½ tbsp cider vinegar
A healthy shake of
 Worcestershire sauce
1 tbsp English or Dijon mustard

A pinch of cayenne pepper
1 heaped tsp redcurrant, crab apple
 or other fruit jelly
2–3 tbsp double cream
Sea salt and freshly ground
 black pepper
Chopped flat-leaf parsley, to finish

Cut the kidneys into quarters and trim out the whitish core.

Set a medium-large frying pan over a high heat. When it is hot, add the lard or oil, followed by the kidneys. Don't stir them straight away – give them a chance to brown a little before tossing them in the pan. After about 1½ minutes, add the brandy (if you're cooking on gas it may ignite, so be careful). Let it bubble and reduce down, then add the cider vinegar, Worcestershire sauce, mustard, cayenne and fruit jelly. Stir to combine.

Now stir in the cream and allow the liquor to bubble and reduce down to a thick coating consistency. Taste and adjust the seasoning or cayenne heat as required. Finish with freshly chopped parsley.

Serve the kidneys with fried bread, or good sourdough toast.

Brains with sage and capers

Britain has a long history of eating all kinds of offal, not just liver and kidneys. Tongue, tripe, feet and brains were once prepared, cooked and enjoyed by families rich and poor. Sadly, times have changed, but this recipe is one of the finest ways I know to eat pig's brains and I'd encourage you to give it a go. Brain has a rich, yet subtle, flavour with a delicate, somewhat creamy, texture. Earthy sage and sharp, salty capers round off this classic sauté.

Serves 2

1 pig's brain
2 bay leaves
6 black peppercorns
A trickle of olive oil
2 tbsp plain flour
20g unsalted butter

12 small sage leaves
1 tbsp baby capers
Juice of ½ lemon
Sea salt and freshly ground
    black pepper

If you have split the pig's head yourself, the brain will be in two halves. Give them a gentle wash in a bowl of cold water. Allow them to soak for 5–10 minutes, then lift out and carefully peel away the dark, frail membrane. It may tear, but do your best to remove it all.

Bring a small pan of water to a simmer and add the bay leaves and peppercorns. Lower in the brain and poach for 4–5 minutes over a very low heat. Lift out the brain on to a plate and allow to cool.

Heat a small frying pan over a medium heat and add the oil. Season the flour with salt and pepper. Dust the brain halves in the seasoned flour, coating them well.

Add the brain to the pan and fry for 2–3 minutes on the first side. Turn the brain and fry for 1 minute on the second side, then add the butter and scatter over the sage leaves and capers. Fry for a further 1–2 minutes, giving the pan an occasional shake, then add a good squeeze of lemon juice. Season with salt and pepper to taste, and serve.

Black pudding Scotch eggs

Never will I tire of eating black pudding and eggs – together or individually. They are what the French call *meilleurs amis*. I like to eat these black pudding Scotch eggs with a good mayonnaise, finished with lots of freshly chopped chives. They're delicious eaten warm, but they're just as good cold, for breakfast.

Makes 6

400g homemade or good-quality
   shop-bought black pudding
200g fatty minced pork
50g fresh white breadcrumbs
1 tbsp chopped parsley
6 medium eggs, at room temperature
Sunflower oil, for deep-frying

Sea salt and freshly ground
   black pepper

For the coating
100g plain flour
1–2 medium eggs
200g coarse fresh white breadcrumbs

Put the black pudding, minced pork, breadcrumbs and parsley into a large bowl and mix until evenly combined, seasoning well with salt and pepper. Divide the mixture into 12 even-sized balls.

Bring a pan of water to the boil, add the 6 eggs and cook for 6 minutes, which should give you a soft-set yolk. Drain the eggs and run them under the cold tap until cool enough to handle. Carefully shell them.

For the coating, set out three bowls. Put the flour into one bowl and season it with salt and pepper. Break an egg into the next and beat it lightly. Tip the coarse breadcrumbs into the third bowl.

Take two of the black pudding balls and flatten them out to rough discs, about 6cm in diameter. Place one disc in the palm of your hand, set a boiled egg in the middle, then top with the second disc. Mould the black pudding around the egg, sealing the joins well. Repeat with the remaining black pudding and eggs.

Coat each Scotch egg with seasoned flour. Next, dip it in the beaten egg (lightly beat in another egg if you need to) and finally roll it in the breadcrumbs. Chill the eggs until you're ready to cook them.

Heat a 5–7cm depth of oil in a deep pan to 175°C, or until hot enough to turn a few breadcrumbs golden in 30–40 seconds. Cook 2 or 3 eggs at a time. Lower them into the oil and fry for 6–8 minutes, turning regularly until golden and crisp. Drain on kitchen paper and leave to stand for 5–10 minutes before tucking in.

Crispy pig's ears
with fennel and lemon mayonnaise

Pig's ears are – and always will be – ears, no matter how tricksy one gets with them, but that's what makes them so great. They're fun, flavoursome and have an appealing texture that's crunchy on the outside with a pleasing, subtle bite within.

Serves 8–10 as a canapé

2 pig's ears, prepared and cleaned
   (see p.119)
2 carrots, peeled and chopped
1 onion, peeled and quartered
2 celery sticks, chopped
2 bay leaves
75g plain flour
2 eggs, lightly beaten
100g fresh coarse breadcrumbs
Sea salt and freshly ground black pepper

For the fennel mayonnaise
½ small garlic clove, peeled
2 large egg yolks
½ tsp English mustard
Finely grated zest and juice of
   1 small lemon
½ tsp toasted fennel seeds, ground
175ml sunflower oil
75ml extra virgin olive or rapeseed oil
A small bunch of fennel tops, chopped

Place the pig's ears in a suitable pan along with the vegetables and bay leaves. Bring to a gentle simmer and put the lid on, partially covering the pan. Cook gently for 2–3 hours, topping up the water as necessary. Once cooked, lift out the pig's ears and allow them to cool. Save the stock to use for other recipes.

Once cooled, cut the ears into 1–2cm wide strips. Season the flour with salt and pepper. Toss the ears in the flour, then in the egg and lastly in the breadcrumbs. Place the pieces of breaded ear in the fridge until you're ready to fry them.

To make the mayonnaise, crush the garlic with a good pinch of salt. In a bowl, mix the garlic with the egg yolks, mustard, lemon zest and juice, fennel seed and some salt and pepper. Combine the oils in a jug, then slowly start whisking into the yolk mix, a few drops at a time to start with, then in a slight trickle, whisking all the time. Once you've added all the oil, you should have a thick, glossy mayo that holds its shape. Add the chopped fennel. Taste and add more salt, pepper, mustard or lemon if required. If the mayo seems too thick, stir in 1–2 tbsp warm water.

To cook, heat a 5–7cm depth of oil in a deep pan to 175°C, or until hot enough to turn a few breadcrumbs golden in 30–40 seconds. Add the pig's ears and deep-fry for 1–2 minutes, or until golden and crisp. Remove and drain on kitchen paper.

Serve at once, with a sprinkling of salt, a squeeze of lemon and the fennel mayo.

Brain McNuggets

We serve these on our Pig in a Day course as an intriguing, fun appetiser. They are rarely refused, which I put down to the two things that have earned them their name – their familiar appearance and bite-sized proportions.

Serves 6–8 as a canapé

1 pig's brain, poached and cooled (as for the recipe on p.154)
2–3 tbsp plain flour
1 egg
75–100g fresh coarse white breadcrumbs
Sunflower oil for shallow-frying

Sea salt and freshly ground black pepper

To serve
Lemon wedges
Flaky sea salt

Take the cooled, poached brain and divide it into 12–16 even pieces, using a sharp knife.

Set out three bowls. Put the flour into one bowl and season it with salt and pepper. Break the egg into the next bowl and beat it lightly. Tip the coarse breadcrumbs into the third bowl.

Dust the brain pieces in the seasoned flour. Now dip them, one by one, in the beaten egg, coating well, then drop them straight into the breadcrumbs to coat all over. Remove to a plate, gently shaking off the excess crumbs. Repeat until all the pieces are coated.

Heat about a 2cm depth of oil in a small pan to 175°C, or until hot enough to turn a few breadcrumbs golden in 30–40 seconds. Fry the breaded brain pieces in batches if necessary, turning occasionally, for about 1 minute until golden brown all over. Remove and drain on kitchen paper. Serve at once, with a squeeze of lemon and a pinch of flaky salt.

Chargrilled kidney wraps
with North African flatbreads

Pig's kidneys have a good flavour and a unique texture and they work well with some pretty pokey spices. Warm cumin and zesty coriander form the base of this fragrant rub, which I like to use on kidneys before chargrilling them. Of course, they can be eaten conventionally with a knife and fork, but if you've got time, knock together a few of these wraps for a fun and delicious way to eat kidneys.

Serves 2

2 very fresh pig's kidneys
2 tsp cumin seeds
2 tsp coriander seeds
2 tsp fennel seeds
1 dried red chilli, finely chopped
2 garlic cloves, peeled and sliced
A trickle of olive oil
Sea salt and freshly ground pepper

For the flatbreads

250g plain white flour, plus extra
   for dusting
250g strong white bread flour
5g active dried yeast
10g fine salt
150ml warm water
175ml natural yoghurt
1 tbsp good olive oil

Serving options
A handful of lettuce leaves,
   roughly shredded
A 4–5cm piece of cucumber,
   sliced
2–3 spring onions, trimmed and
   thinly sliced
3–4 ripe tomatoes, sliced
A handful of mint leaves, roughly
   shredded
Natural yoghurt

Start by making the flatbread dough well ahead to allow time for rising. Mix the flours, yeast, salt, water and yoghurt together in a bowl to form a sticky dough, then add the olive oil and mix it in. Turn the dough out on to a clean surface and knead until smooth and silky.

Shape the dough into a round and place in a clean bowl. Cover the bowl with cling film or a damp tea towel and leave the dough to rise until doubled in size – at least 1 hour.

Deflate or 'knock back' the dough, then, if you have time, leave it to rise a second or third time. This improves the flavour.

Tear off pieces of dough, the size of golf balls. Shape them, one at a time, into rounds, then, using plenty of flour, roll out to a 3–4mm thickness and leave to rest for a few minutes.

Meanwhile, heat a large heavy-based frying pan over a high heat. When the pan is really hot, lay the first bread in it. After a minute, or possibly less, the bread should be puffy and starting to char on the bottom. Flip the flatbread over and cook for a further 1–2 minutes. Repeat to cook the rest of the dough. Keep the wraps warm in a tea towel.

On a board and using your sharpest knife, carefully halve the kidneys horizontally and remove the tough white core, using the tip of your knife. Cut each kidney half into broad strips, about 2cm thick.

Put the dry spices, including the chilli, in a small frying pan set over a medium heat. Toast the spices until fragrant and just starting to pop. Tip them into a mortar and grind with the pestle to a fairly fine texture.

Toss the pieces of kidney in the ground spices, then add the garlic, some salt and pepper and a good trickle of olive oil and toss again. If time, let the kidneys marinate in the spice for half an hour or so before cooking.

When you're ready to cook, place a medium chargrill pan over a high heat. Lay the kidney pieces in the pan and cook for 3–4 minutes on each side or until just cooked through.

Assemble your wraps in whichever way you like. I generally include some crunchy salad leaves, cooling cucumber slices and a good dollop of thick natural yoghurt, which takes the edge off the spice.

Barbecued pork chump
with herbs

The chump is a favourite cut of mine. It is slightly more tender and flavoursome than the leg and somewhat fattier and more forgiving than the loin. Chump chops are fantastic, but chump makes a magic roasting joint as well. This can be cooked conventionally in your oven but the results are all the more splendid when it's cooked gently over the glowing embers of a charcoal barbecue. The heat from the coals must not be too fierce, or the meat may burn before it's cooked through.

Serves 3–4

1 whole pork chump, boned and
   skinned, leaving a layer of fat
A small handful each of parsley,
   tarragon, basil, mint and chives
2 tbsp olive oil

Finely grated zest of 1 lemon
1 garlic clove, peeled and grated
A pinch of dried chilli flakes (optional)
Sea salt and freshly ground
   black pepper

Light your barbecue about an hour before you plan to cook the pork.

Meanwhile, place the chump on a board, fat side up. Use a sharp knife to score the fat almost down to the meat in a crisscross fashion.

Pick the leafy herbs from their stalks and chop them relatively finely. Gather up the chives and slice them thinly. Place all the herbs in a bowl and combine with the olive oil, lemon zest, grated garlic, chilli, if using, and some salt and pepper.

Rub half this herby mixture all over the pork, making sure it gets into all the nooks and crannies. Place the pork on the barbecue grid and begin the cooking process. Turn the pork regularly, making sure you cook it on all sides. With a medium heat under the joint, it should be cooked through in 25–30 minutes.

If at any point the pork seems to be colouring up too much, remove it and allow the heat to reduce a little before replacing the chump. When cooked, remove the pork to a plate.

Take the remaining herb mixture and rub it all over the pork (without burning your fingers). This will give it a fresh, fragrant finish. Allow the pork to rest for 10 minutes before serving in slices, with new potatoes and ripe tomatoes.

Tenderloin with courgettes,
dill, mint and spring onions

Pork tenderloin is a delicate and lean cut. I love its open, tender grain and the fact that it is so simple to cook. Sadly, in relation to the rest of the pig, the tenderloin is really quite small, so you must make the most of it when you come to cook it. This salad – which is full of vibrant, fresh herby flavours – does it justice.

Serves 2

1 pork tenderloin, about 300g
2 firm, medium courgettes
2–3 tbsp good olive oil, plus
    a trickle to serve
1 garlic clove, peeled and sliced
A small bunch of mint, leaves only
A small bunch of chives
    (with flowers if available)

A handful of dill, plus extra sprigs
    to serve
A small bunch of spring onions,
    trimmed and sliced
Juice of 1 lemon
Sea salt and freshly ground
    black pepper

Preheat the grill to high. Trim the tenderloin of any sinew or membrane, using the tip of a sharp knife.

Slice the courgettes into rounds, a fraction thicker than a £1 coin. Put them into a bowl and add the olive oil, garlic and some salt and pepper. Tumble everything together, then lay out in a single layer over a large baking tray. Take the tenderloin and rub it around the bowl, to gather up the seasoning and oil that has been left behind. Nestle this on to the tray with the courgettes.

Grill the courgettes and tenderloin for 6–10 minutes on each side until the courgettes are golden and tender and the meat is just cooked through. (The cooking time will depend on the efficiency of your grill and how close everything is to the element.)

Tip the cooked courgettes into a clean bowl and put the tenderloin on a board to rest. Chop the mint, chives and dill together and add to the courgettes with the sliced spring onion and lemon juice. Toss to combine.

Slice the tenderloin into 1cm thick pieces, on an angle. Turn the pork through the warm courgettes and season again with salt and pepper to taste. Divide equally between two large plates. Finish with a few sprigs of fresh dill, some chive flowers, if you have them, and an extra trickle of olive oil.

Tenderloin with peaches,
honey and almonds

We all know pork and apples go together, but I really love this alternative fruity pairing. It's a light and refreshing way to eat pork. The kebabs cook beautifully on the barbecue, or equally well under the grill. Be generous with the mint and honey, as they really pull the dish together.

Serves 2

1 pork tenderloin, about 300g
4 almost-ripe peaches
1 tbsp olive oil
2 tbsp runny honey

2–3 tbsp toasted flaked almonds
2 tbsp chopped mint
Sea salt and freshly ground
    black pepper

Heat up the barbecue, or preheat your grill to high.

Trim the tenderloin of any sinew or membrane, using the tip of a sharp knife. Slice it into rounds, about 2–3cm thick. Halve and stone the peaches, then cut them into large chunks.

Take 4 wooden or metal kebab skewers. Thread the tenderloin rounds and peach chunks alternately on to each skewer; you should fit 3 pieces of each on to each skewer. Lay the kebabs on a baking tray, trickle with good olive oil and season well with salt and pepper.

Place the kebabs on the barbecue or under the hot grill and cook, turning regularly, for 4–6 minutes or until the pork is just cooked through. Finish with a good trickle of runny honey, the toasted almonds and some freshly chopped mint.

Pork stock

A well-made pork stock is just as good as any beef or chicken stock and it's something we make all the time in the River Cottage kitchen. It forms the basis of lots of our sauces, reductions, soups and stews. Save all your pork bones – they freeze really well. Roasting the bones before you make your stock will give it a wonderful deep flavour.

Makes 2.5–3 litres

3kg pork bones, roughly chopped, plus any lean meat trimmings you have
3 onions, peeled and quartered
4 large carrots, peeled and halved
3–4 celery sticks, roughly chopped
1 whole garlic bulb, halved horizontally
A few black peppercorns
A few fennel seeds
6 bay leaves
3–4 sprigs of thyme (optional)
A few parsley stalks (optional)
Sea salt and freshly ground black pepper

Preheat the oven to 200°C/Gas mark 6.

Place the pork bones in a large roasting tray and season them well with salt and pepper. Roast for 40–45 minutes, turning once, until golden and caramelised. Using tongs, transfer the roasted bones to a large stockpot.

Pour off any excess fat from the roasting tray, then place the tray over a low heat and add a glass of water to deglaze. Stir and scrape up the sticky, sweet caramelised bits from the bottom of the tray with a wooden spoon. Add this liquor to the stockpot, along with the vegetables, garlic, peppercorns, fennel seeds and herbs, then pour in enough fresh water to cover everything.

Bring to a gentle simmer and cook, uncovered, for at least 3 hours – and up to 5. Top up the water once or twice, if necessary. Strain the stock through a fine sieve, leave it to cool, then chill. You can freeze your stock in batches – that way you'll always have some on hand.

Chorizo and bean soup
with nettles and sourdough toast

This rustic country soup is hearty and warming. I like to use homemade pork stock as it adds a real depth of flavour to the dish. My recipe for chorizo (given as a variation of saucisson sec, on pp.219–21) is perfect for this soup, or you can use good-quality or organic shop-bought chorizo, if you can find it. Nettles, which can be picked in spring and then again in the autumn, give this soup a great twist – but when they're out of season, you can use kale or chard instead.

Serves 4

150g dried cannellini beans, soaked overnight in cold water
A dash of good extra virgin olive oil
200g chorizo sausage, sliced into rounds
1 large or 2 smaller onions, peeled and finely sliced
A sprig of rosemary
4 garlic cloves, peeled and finely sliced

1 litre pork stock (p.171) or chicken stock
4 slices of 2–3-day-old sourdough, or similar good bread
A colander full of young nettle tops, washed and roughly chopped
Sea salt and freshly ground black pepper

Drain the soaked beans and tip them into a saucepan. Cover with fresh water and bring to a simmer, then cook for 45 minutes or until tender. Drain and set aside.

Warm a heavy-based saucepan over a medium heat and add a trickle of olive oil. Add the sliced chorizo and fry for 2–3 minutes to release some of the oil, then add the onion, rosemary, cooked beans and garlic (saving the end bits to rub on your toasts). Season with salt and pepper, then continue to cook, without colouring the onion, for a further 5 minutes.

Pour in the stock, stir well, and then bring to a low simmer. Simmer gently for 15–20 minutes.

Meanwhile, toast the pieces of sourdough on each side, trickle with olive oil, rub with the reserved garlic and sprinkle with flaky sea salt.

Add the nettle tops to the pan and cook for a further 5 minutes. Taste the soup and adjust the seasoning.

To serve, ladle the soup into large soup plates or bowls and serve with the toasted sourdough. Finish with a trickle of extra virgin olive oil, if you like.

Terrine of pig's trotters
and ham hock

You can cure your own ham hocks very easily at home (see p.229). Alternatively, uncooked hocks of cured gammon can be bought from most good butchers.

Serves 8–10

2 pig's trotters, cut long
1 large or 2 smaller ham hocks, about 1kg in total
2 onions, peeled and quartered
2 celery sticks
2 large carrots, peeled
1 whole garlic bulb, halved horizontally
4 or 5 sprigs of thyme

4 bay leaves
A small bunch of flat-leaf parsley, leaves only, chopped
2 tsp wholegrain mustard
Sea salt and freshly ground black pepper

Equipment
1-litre terrine or similar container(s)

Wash the pig's trotter pieces under cold running water. Put them in a large heavy-based saucepan along with the ham hocks and the vegetables, garlic, thyme and bay leaves, packing everything into the pan as snugly as possible. Pour over just enough fresh water to cover the ingredients.

Place the pan over a medium heat and bring to a simmer. Skim off any scum that rises to the surface. Turn the heat down to its lowest setting and simmer as gently as possible for 2–2½ hours.

Remove the ham hock and trotters – they should be so tender that the skin and meat fall away from the bone. Set the meat aside to cool. Strain the cooking liquor through a muslin-lined sieve into a clean pan. Bring to the boil and boil until the liquor has reduced by half.

Meanwhile, pick the skin and meat from the pig's trotters and shred the ham from the bone. Roughly chop the meat and skin so it's all of a regular size – roughly 1cm pieces. Place in a clean bowl.

Pour the reduced stock over the meat. Add the parsley and mustard and season to taste with salt and pepper. Pack the mixture into a terrine or similar container (or into several ramekins). Refrigerate for 6–8 hours or overnight.

Serve the terrine cut into generous slices, with pickled baby cucumbers, good piccalilli (p.205) or a few pickled eggs and bread.

Tongue with salsa verde
and lentils

Tongue has a great texture: it is deeply meaty with a unique richness. I like to brine the pig's tongues for a day or two before cooking them. They work really well with a sharp, clean sauce, such as salsa verde, and some nutty lentils.

Serves 4

For the quick brine
300g fine salt
1 litre water

For the tongues
4 pig's tongues
1 onion, peeled and halved
2 carrots, peeled and roughly chopped
2–3 celery sticks
2 bay leaves
A few parsley stalks
2–3 sprigs of thyme
200g Puy lentils

For the salsa verde
A large bunch of flat-leaf parsley
A bunch of mint
1 tbsp capers, rinsed and chopped
6–8 anchovy fillets, finely chopped
1 small garlic clove, peeled and finely chopped
1 tbsp Dijon mustard
2 tsp vinegar
3–4 tbsp extra virgin olive oil
Sea salt and freshly ground black pepper

For the brine, put the salt and water into a big bowl and whisk to encourage the salt to dissolve. Add the tongues, weighing them down if necessary to keep them submerged. Refrigerate for 48 hours.

Remove the tongues from the brine, rinse under cold running water, then place in a pan with the veg and herbs. Cover with water and simmer gently for 2½–3 hours until tender and yielding, topping up the water as necessary. Lift out the tongues and, while still warm, peel off the coarse outer skin. Strain and reserve the stock.

To make the salsa verde, finely chop the parsley and mint leaves and place in a bowl with the capers, anchovies and garlic. Add the mustard and vinegar, then enough olive oil to loosen the salsa to a spoonable consistency. Season with salt and pepper.

Rinse the lentils under cold running water for a minute then place in a pan. Pour over the stock (reserved from cooking the tongues). Bring to a simmer and cook for 20–25 minutes, or until the lentils are tender. A few minutes before they will be ready, add the tongues to the pan to warm through. Drain in a colander.

Serve each tongue with a pile of lentils and a generous spoonful of salsa verde.

Brawn

The French name for this dish is *fromage de tête*, meaning 'head cheese'. I don't think that term quite does justice to such a delicacy. Brawn was one of the first dishes I made for Hugh when I started working at River Cottage nearly 10 years ago. For me, it sums up everything that's good about thrifty, holistic cookery. You start out with something that's considered a cheap cut and turn it into a seriously delicious and unique dish. A good brawn is a balance of meat, fat and skin in the right proportions. If you have a very fatty pig's head, you wouldn't simply put all the fat in. Likewise, if your pig has very big ears, as with a Large Black, you may not want to put all the ear in – it would throw the textural balance out, making your brawn altogether too eary. When you're making brawn at home, consider your own preferences before putting the terrine together. You may like it coarse and fatty, or lean and well shredded, for example.

Makes 2 terrines; each serves 8–10

1 pig's head, including tongue
1 or 2 pig's trotters
1 pig's tail (optional)
2 onions, peeled and quartered
2 celery sticks
2 carrots
1 whole garlic bulb
A small bunch of thyme
A handful of parsley stalks
2 bay leaves
A few fennel stalks
2 tsp mixed peppercorns
2 tsp cloves

2 tsp coriander seeds
A large handful of parsley leaves, chopped
Juice of ½ lemon
½ tsp ground mace
Sea salt and freshly ground black pepper

Equipment
Large stockpot
2 x 1-litre terrines or similar container(s)

Prepare the pig's head as described on p.119. Put the pieces of head in a large pan, along with the tongue, trotters and tail, if using, onions, celery, carrots, garlic and herbs. Tie up the whole spices in a piece of muslin and add this to the pan. Add enough water to cover and bring slowly to a gentle simmer.

Cook, uncovered, at a very gentle simmer for about 4 hours, or until all the meat is completely tender and coming away from the bones. For the first 30 minutes of cooking, skim off any scum that rises to the surface. Top up the pan as necessary during cooking if the water level drops.

When cooked, lift out the pieces of head and leave until cool enough to handle. Pick the meat, skin and fat off the bones and cut the ears into thin strips. Sometimes you get a tougher base to the ears; if this is the case, don't include these parts.

Make piles of the different types of meat, piles of the clean white fat and skin (free of any stubble) and a pile of ear pieces. You can then see what's going into your brawn and what you don't want in it. Watch out for the glands underneath the cheeks and any sinew or membrane or thin bone pieces; these bits should not go in. Peel off and discard the coarse skin from the tongue.

Cut and shred all the bits of meat, including the fat, skin and tongue, and toss them together in a large bowl with the chopped parsley and lemon juice. Season to taste with salt, pepper and mace.

Remove the herbs, onions and spice bag from the cooking liquor and strain it through a fine sieve or, better still, muslin. Pour 2 litres of this strained stock into a large pan and boil to reduce to about 500ml; this will take about 20–25 minutes. While still hot, stir half this liquid into the chopped meat mixture. Pile the mixture into terrines or similar dishes, then top equally with the remaining stock.

Refrigerate the brawn for at least 24 hours, ideally 48 to give it time to mature. Eat with good bread, mustard and pickled cucumbers, or some peppery rocket leaves.

Pork with leeks and pancetta
in cider and cream

I make this rich autumnal dish with cubed leg of pork. The cream and pancetta keep the sauce lovely and moist so the leg meat doesn't dry out, as it sometimes tends to. The rosemary, with its heady notes, works beautifully with the pork and a good spoonful of grainy mustard gives the dish sweetness and depth.

Serves 4

35g butter
3 large leeks, trimmed, well washed
   and thinly sliced
1 tbsp lard or olive oil
200g pancetta or bacon, cut into
   chunky cubes
3–4 tbsp plain flour
1kg leg (or chump) of pork, cubed

500ml medium cider
300ml double cream
2 sprigs of rosemary
1 tbsp wholegrain mustard
Sea salt and freshly ground
   black pepper
1 heaped tbsp chopped parsley,
   to finish

Heat the butter in a large casserole or saucepan set over a medium heat. Add the leeks and a little seasoning and sweat them gently for about 10 minutes until soft and silky.

Meanwhile, heat the lard or oil in a frying pan over a medium-high heat and add the pancetta or bacon cubes. Cook for 5–6 minutes, or until well browned, then add to the leeks in the casserole and set aside, leaving behind some of the rendered fat in the frying pan.

Season the flour with salt and pepper. Put the frying pan back over a medium heat. Toss the pork leg pieces lightly in the seasoned flour, then add to the hot pan and brown well all over. Now add the pork to the bacon and leeks in the casserole.

Deglaze the frying pan with the cider, allowing it to bubble for a few moments while you scrape the base of the pan to release any caramelised meaty residue, then add this liquid to the casserole dish. Pour in the cream and add the rosemary. Bring to a simmer and cook gently, uncovered, for 1–1½ hours or until the meat is very tender. Top up with water if the sauce becomes a little too reduced.

When the pork is cooked, stir in the mustard and season with salt and pepper to taste. Finish with a generous sprinkling of chopped parsley. Serve with potatoes, mashed or sautéed, and a sharply dressed crisp green salad.

Pork and pumpkin curry

This is a really good curry for a Friday or Saturday night – it's one I often make at home when I have a few friends over. It can be cooked a day or two in advance and is often better for it. It freezes well too, so you might like to make a big batch to stock up the freezer with a few meals.

Serves 6

750g lean shoulder or leg of pork
750g pumpkin
2 tbsp lard or oil
1 large onion, peeled and thinly sliced
200ml coconut milk
Sea salt and freshly ground
    black pepper

To finish
A good handful of coriander, leaves
    only, roughly chopped
A generous squeeze of lime juice

For the curry paste
4 cloves
1 star anise
1 tsp black peppercorns
3 tsp cumin seeds
3 tsp coriander seeds
10 cardamom pods, seeds extracted
50g fresh root ginger
4 garlic cloves
1 small onion
1 tbsp curry powder
½ tsp salt

Start by making the curry paste. Using a pestle and mortar, grind the cloves, star anise, peppercorns and the cumin, coriander and cardamom seeds together to a fairly fine texture. Peel and roughly chop the ginger, garlic and onion, then put into a blender with the ground spices, curry powder and salt. Blitz, adding just enough water to form a purée.

Cut the pork into 3–4cm cubes. Peel and deseed the pumpkin and cut into large cubes; set aside.

Heat the lard or oil in a large, wide pan. Season the pork with salt and pepper, add to the pan and cook until well browned. Turn down the heat a little and add the curry paste. Cook for 2 minutes, stirring regularly to ensure the spices don't burn.

Add the onion to the pan and cook for a few minutes until softened, then add the pumpkin and cook for a further 5 minutes. Pour in enough water to just cover the pork and pumpkin. Put the lid on the pan and simmer over a low heat for 20–30 minutes until the pork is tender.

Stir in the coconut milk and heat through. Adjust the seasoning if necessary, then stir through the chopped coriander. Finish with a good squeeze of lime.

Bacon with beans and squid

I can't think of anything I'd rather eat on a chilly winter's night than this rich, hearty stew, perfumed with lemon and bay. The richness comes from the bacon, which is cooked gently alongside the squid until both are giving and tender. If you are not a fan of squid, you can simply leave it out.

Serves 4

250g dried haricot beans, soaked overnight in cold water
350g piece of home-cured bacon or good streaky bacon, boned (skin on)
A little oil or lard
4 small or 2 medium squid, cleaned
1 large onion, peeled and sliced
4 garlic cloves, peeled and sliced
A small bunch of thyme

4 bay leaves
Finely pared zest and juice of 1 lemon
400g tin chopped tomatoes
Sea salt and freshly ground black pepper

To serve
Fennel tops or flat-leaf parsley
Extra virgin olive oil

Drain and rinse the beans, then tip into a medium saucepan and add fresh water to cover. Bring to the boil and cook for 10 minutes, then lower the heat, cover and simmer for about an hour, or until the beans are just tender. Drain and set aside.

Preheat the oven to 120°C/Gas mark ½. Cut the bacon into 4–5cm cubes. Place a large heavy-based flameproof casserole over a medium-high heat. Add the oil or lard, followed by the pieces of bacon and cook them on all sides until caramelised and golden: this will take 4–5 minutes. Remove the bacon pieces to a plate.

Slice the squid into 1–2cm rounds and the tentacles into several pieces. Drop the squid into the casserole and brown all over for 3–4 minutes. Take out the squid and set aside with the bacon. Lower the heat under the casserole to medium.

Add the onion, garlic, thyme, bay leaves and lemon zest to the casserole and cook, stirring often, until the onions start to soften, about 6–8 minutes. Return the bacon to the casserole and add the squid, tinned tomatoes, beans and about 300ml water. Put the lid on and place in the oven. Cook for 3 hours, stirring once every hour and checking it's not getting too dry. If it is, add a splash more water. After the allotted time, take a piece of pork out to check – it should be incredibly tender.

Taste and adjust the seasoning, and skim off any excess fat from the surface if you like. Finish this fragrant dish with freshly chopped fennel tops or parsley, a trickle of good olive oil and the juice from the zested lemon.

Stuffed pig's trotters
with ceps, bacon and potato

I once saw Pierre Koffmann bone out a pig's trotter in under a minute. It was good to watch the master at work but you don't have to be so accomplished to have a go. With a little practice and determination you should be able to manage it – just give yourself a good 10 minutes first time round. This is my version of the classic stuffed trotter dish made famous by chef Koffman.

Serves 4

4 pig's back trotters, cut long
   and boned (see pp.114–15)
1 large onion, peeled and sliced
2 carrots, peeled and chopped
A glass of white wine
300ml pork stock (p.171)
   or chicken stock
4 sprigs of thyme

For the potato stuffing
2 large floury potatoes, peeled
   and cubed
100g dried ceps
20g butter
A dash of olive oil
75g streaky bacon or pancetta, diced
1 small onion, peeled and finely
   chopped
A small bunch of parsley, leaves only,
   chopped
Sea salt and freshly ground
   black pepper

Preheat the oven to 160°C/Gas mark 3.

Place the trotters in a heavy casserole dish with the onion, carrots, wine, stock and thyme. Cover and cook in the oven for 2½–3 hours.

Meanwhile, for the stuffing, add the potatoes to a pan of salted water, bring to the boil and cook until tender. Soak the dried ceps in a bowl of warm water for 10–15 minutes, then drain, reserving the liquor. Once the potatoes are cooked, drain and then return them to the pan. Mash well with the butter and set aside.

Place a frying pan over a medium heat and add a dash of oil, followed by the bacon or pancetta. Cook for 5–6 minutes or until just starting to colour. Add the onion and ceps and continue to cook, tossing regularly, until the onion is soft and the bacon is crisping slightly. Season with salt and pepper and add the chopped parsley.

Add the bacon and cep mixture to the mashed potato and combine thoroughly. Leave to cool, then chill.

Lift the trotters out of the casserole on to a board. Strain and reserve the cooking liquor, discarding the vegetables and herbs.

To prepare the trotters for stuffing, open out the tender skin that surrounded the bone you removed. Divide the potato and cep mixture into 4 portions and fill each trotter, carefully encasing the stuffing as you go. Wrap each stuffed trotter tightly in foil and refrigerate until set.

When ready to eat, preheat the oven to 200°C/Gas mark 6. Place the stuffed trotters in a roasting tray with 2 glasses of water and warm through in the hot oven for 20–25 minutes. Skim off any fat from the reserved trotter cooking liquor, then combine with the cep soaking liquor. Pour into a pan, bring to the boil and boil steadily until reduced by two-thirds. Season with salt and pepper to taste.

Carefully remove the foil from each stuffed trotter and place on warmed plates. Spoon over the sauce and serve with buttered Savoy cabbage.

Pig's spleen with red wine,
marjoram and onions

The spleen is an organ found in almost all vertebrate animals – including man, and pigs. It's not dissimilar to liver in flavour although it has a lighter, more open texture. If you keep your own pigs, make sure you ask the abattoir for the spleen back when you send them to slaughter. I like it slow-cooked with lots of red wine, marjoram, bacon and onions.

Serves 2

1 pig's spleen, caul fat removed
   and reserved
2 thick slices of streaky bacon
1 tbsp chopped marjoram
½ tbsp extra virgin olive oil
A small knob of butter
2 large onions, peeled and thinly sliced

2 garlic cloves, peeled and thinly sliced
2 bay leaves
2 glasses of red wine
300ml pork stock (p.171) or chicken
   stock
Sea salt and freshly ground
   black pepper

Preheat the oven to 160°C/Gas mark 3.

Lay the spleen down on a board and season it well all over with salt and pepper. Lay the bacon over the spleen and scatter with a little chopped marjoram. Roll the spleen up on itself, encasing the bacon inside. Take a piece of caul fat and encase the rolled spleen.

Place a medium-small casserole over a medium heat, then add the oil and butter. Once the butter has melted, add the wrapped, rolled spleen. Gently brown all over for 6–8 minutes then remove to a plate.

Add the onions to the casserole and cook gently for 10–15 minutes until softened, stirring regularly so they don't burn. Add the garlic, bay leaves and remaining marjoram and cook for a further 3–4 minutes. Now turn up the heat, add the wine and bring to a simmer. Return the spleen to the casserole, along with the stock. Put the lid on and cook in the oven for 1½–2 hours.

Take the casserole out of the oven and remove the spleen. Taste the red wine sauce and adjust the seasoning if required. For a more intense flavour, you can pop the casserole on the hob and boil the liquor until reduced by half.

To serve, slice the spleen into rounds and divide between warmed plates. Spoon over the tender onions and red wine sauce. Serve with mash or parsnip purée.

Pig's tail and damsons

Sometimes I will put the pig's tail into my brawn (see p.178), as it's a good way to incorporate it into a dish. But sometimes I'll serve it solo – crispy and crunchy – with a damson or plum compote. It's fun, and I find people always enjoy eating something a little unusual.

Serves 2

2 pig's tails
A trickle of olive oil
8–10 damsons or 4–5 small ripe
  plums, halved and stoned
1–2 tsp sugar

A small knob of butter
Sea salt and freshly ground
  black pepper
Fennel flowers (if available),
  to finish

First you need to remove most of the bone from the tails. Place one on a board and split it down its length with the point of a sharp knife. You don't have to go all the way to the tip of the tail, just about halfway down will be fine. Now carefully trim out the bone from within by tracing the knife around it. The thinner section of tail bone can be left in. Repeat with the other tail.

Place the boned tails in a pan of boiling water and simmer for 45 minutes–1 hour. Remove them from the pan and allow to steam off in a colander while you preheat the oven to 200°C/Gas mark 6.

Place the pig's tails on a baking tray. Season with salt and pepper, and trickle over some olive oil. Roast in the oven for 25 minutes or until crisp and crackly.

Put the damsons into a small pan with the sugar and butter and cook gently over a medium-low heat for 3–4 minutes until just starting to soften. Taste and adjust the sweetness if necessary.

Serve a spoonful of the damson compote alongside each tail. I like to scatter over a few fennel flowers if I have them – they add a lovely aniseedy twang. The small amount of bone left in the tail becomes tender enough to crunch up, so you can eat the whole thing.

Roast pork loin
with black pudding and beetroot

This recipe is fantastic with homemade black pudding (p.137) but if you haven't had a chance to get your hands bloody yet, you can get great black pudding from a variety of good producers and butchers. Black pudding makes a rich and comforting stuffing and keeps the pork loin sweet and moist.

It's best if your loin has been cut with a slightly longer tail; by this I mean the amount of belly left on the loin joint once it has been divided. This makes it much easier to roll the joint once it is stuffed. If you're not preparing your own pork, ask your butcher to do this for you.

Serves 6

A piece of boned loin of pork,
    about 2kg
250g black pudding
A small bunch of thyme

2 tbsp olive oil, to trickle
6–8 small beetroot
Sea salt and freshly ground
    black pepper

Preheat the oven to 220°C/Gas mark 7.

Ensure the skin of the pork is dry to the touch. Score the skin using a very sharp blade, such as a Stanley knife, making long cuts about 2cm apart all over the skin, going into the fat, but not down to the meat (see p.101).

Place the loin skin side down on a board. Use a sharp knife to make a shallow cut about 2cm deep along the length of the loin, just above where the eye of the meat meets the very top of the belly. Open up the meat so it's nice and flat, and season it all over with salt and pepper.

If the black pudding has been made and cooked in a traditional beef runner, remove the skin; if it's been made in a terrine you won't need to. Stuff the black pudding into the cut you made along the length of the loin, and press any excess over the meat, along its length.

Pick the leaves from the thyme (save the stalks) and roughly chop them. Scatter the thyme leaves over the pork and black pudding. Trickle the whole lot with good olive oil. Roll up the joint, enclosing the stuffing, and tie firmly, using the butcher's knot (see pp.102–3).

Place the pork loin in a roasting tray and add the beetroot. Scatter over the thyme stalks and season everything, particularly the skin, well with sea salt and a twist of

pepper. Put the joint into the oven and roast for 20–25 minutes. You should see the skin start to pop and blister, which is a good sign if, like me, you're a fan of crisp crackling.

Lower the oven setting to 170°C/Gas mark 3 and pour a glass of water into the roasting tray around (but not over) the meat. Return the meat to the oven and roast for a further 1 hour. It is a good idea to use a cook's temperature probe to check that the meat is cooked. This should register 72°C but not higher, as above this temperature the pork will dry out slightly. Transfer both the pork and beetroot to a warm dish to rest.

If you find you have less than perfect crackling, you can remove the skin and pop it either into a hot oven for a further 5–10 minutes or under a hot grill. Keep an eye on it though, as it can burn easily.

Slice the pork thickly and serve on warmed plates with the rich roasting juices, crackling and roasted beetroot. I like to accompany this with a simple green salad.

Simple roast pork belly
with fennel and coriander seeds

This is my foolproof, pared-back recipe for roast pork belly – 'straight up'. Belly is almost certainly one of my desert island pork cuts, due largely to its perfect balance of lean to fat to crackling. This is, quite simply, the best way to cook it.

Serves 4–6

2 tsp fennel seeds
2 tsp coriander seeds
1.5–2kg thick end of pork belly,
   bone in, with nice dry skin

A splash of white wine, cider or water,
   for the gravy
Sea salt and freshly ground
   black pepper

Preheat the oven to 200°C/Gas mark 6.

Toast the seeds in a small dry pan over a medium heat until fragrant and beginning to pop. Grind them coarsely with a pestle.

Score the skin of the pork (see p.101) if it hasn't been done already. Don't cut down into the meat, just into the fat. Place the pork in a suitably sized roasting tin and rub all over with salt and the crushed fennel and coriander.

Place in the oven and cook for 25–30 minutes, then turn the heat down to 160°C/Gas mark 3 and add half a glass of water to the roasting tin around the meat. Roast for a further 2 hours.

Remove the pork from the oven and allow it to rest while you turn your attention to the simplest of roasting juice gravies. Spoon off the fat from the surface of the liquor, then set the roasting tin over a medium heat. Add a splash of white wine, cider or water and bring to a simmer. Stir well and season to taste with salt and pepper. Pass the liquor through a fine sieve and keep warm.

Carve the pork into thick slices, across the grain. Serve with the crackling and gravy, carrots and mustard.

Sticky ribs

This is the easiest sticky rib recipe you'll ever make, but I'd like to think one of the best! The ribs are cooked slowly with garlic, ginger, chilli and soy until beautifully tender and the sauce is rich and finger-stickingly good. The secret is the balance of sweet and sour. I use fresh apple juice and a good-quality cider vinegar to achieve this and they both add a fruity twang to the sauce.

Serves 2–4

1kg pork spare ribs, cut from the belly and/or from the boned loin

For the marinade
4 large garlic cloves, peeled and sliced
1 thumb-sized piece of ginger, peeled and finely chopped or grated

4 tbsp soy sauce
4 tbsp cider vinegar
1 red chilli, deseeded and sliced
2 tbsp soft brown sugar
1 tbsp sesame seeds
125ml apple juice

Preheat the oven to 120°C/Gas ½.

Cut the ribs into manageable pieces; for this task you'll need a cleaver and possibly a butcher's saw. I like them 3–4 ribs thick and 8–10cm in length.

For the marinade, combine all the ingredients in a bowl.

Place the prepared ribs in a large roasting tray or baking dish, pour over the marinade, shake them up a bit, then cover the entire tray with foil, sealing it tightly around the edges. Place the tray in the oven and cook for 2–2½ hours. The ribs should be tender and giving, with a deeply flavoured sticky sauce. Serve with ales and films!

Pulled pork

I remember Hugh teaching me that the secret to really good pulled pork is the oven temperature: it's crucial that it's not too hot. A whole pork shoulder is made up of a variety of different muscle sets, some leaner than others. The leaner ones will dry out at temperatures that don't affect fattier areas. The ultimate goal is to have everything beautifully moist and giving. This is my recipe for the kind of pulled pork you can serve hot in a sandwich at a party, or have with roast potatoes and apple sauce on a Sunday, or in a hash with eggs and mushrooms for breakfast.

Serves 12–15

1 whole shoulder of pork on the bone (about 7–8 kg)
3 onions, peeled and halved
6 carrots, peeled and cut into chunks
4 celery sticks, halved
1–2 fennel bulbs, quartered (optional)

A bunch of mixed herbs, such as sage, thyme, fennel, rosemary and bay
1 whole garlic bulb, halved horizontally
2 glasses of water
Salt and freshly ground black pepper

Preheat the oven to 220°C/Gas mark 7.

Place the whole pork shoulder in a large, deep roasting tin (don't worry if the hock hangs over the edge). Score the skin with a Stanley knife (see p.101) from the top of the shoulder right down to the bottom. Now rub it all over with salt and pepper.

Roast the pork in the oven for 35–40 minutes to get the crackling going. Once it's golden and crackly, remove the pork and lift it, carefully, on to a board.

Add the veg, herbs and garlic to the roasting tin and pour on the water, then return the pork. Now cover the pork with foil, crimping the edges super-tight, to keep the steam in. Return the tin to the oven and turn the setting down to 95°C, Gas ¼. Cook the pork in this very low oven for 12–14 hours (overnight, for convenience).

Take the tin from the oven and remove the foil from the pork. You can either bring the shoulder to the table and let everyone 'pull' their own pork or do it for them. Lift off the crackling, which will need to be crisped in a hot oven, for 5–10 minutes. Take two forks and start pulling tender chunks of meat away from the bone – it should slip off. Pile the pulled pork into a clean, deep, ovenproof serving dish.

Strain the roasting juices, herbs, garlic and veg through a sieve into a warmed bowl, pressing the veg to extract all the flavour. Stir the strained liquor well, then trickle 4–5 ladlefuls over the meat. Season generously with salt and pepper and serve.

Slow-roast pork belly
with chargrilled asparagus and mint

I really like this combination of crunchy, salty crackling, charred soft asparagus, tender succulent pork belly and cool mint. I generally assemble it as a warm salad, but it could just as easily be plated up in a traditional main-course manner. It's a fine spring lunch.

Serves 4

**About 1kg piece of thick-end
pork belly**
A little olive oil
5–6 sprigs of thyme
24 asparagus spears

A small handful of mint leaves
Juice of ½ lemon, or to taste
**Sea salt and freshly ground
black pepper**

To give you the best chance of great crackling, ensure the skin of the pork is nice and dry. I always leave it uncovered in the fridge until I'm ready to cook it.

Preheat the oven to 220°C/Gas mark 7.

Score the skin of the pork (see p.101) if it hasn't been done already. Place the belly in a suitable-sized roasting tin. Rub the skin and underside of the belly with salt, pepper and a little olive oil. Tuck the thyme sprigs in and around the meat. Roast the pork in the oven for 25–30 minutes.

Add a glass of water to the roasting tin, pouring it around (not over) the meat, lower the oven setting to 165°C/Gas mark 3 and cook for 2–2½ hours, or until the meat is giving and coming away from the bone in tender pieces and the skin has crackled to an irresistible golden brown. If the crackling is reluctant to 'crackle', carefully remove it from the pork belly and put it back into the oven at 220°C/Gas mark 7 until it starts to pop. Top up the tin with a little water if it's drying out.

Leave the pork to rest, uncovered, in a warm place for 20 minutes. Meanwhile, set a chargrill pan over a high heat. Toss the asparagus spears in a trickle of olive oil and season them with salt and pepper. When the pan is hot, add the asparagus and cook, turning as necessary, for 3–4 minutes, or until cooked through.

To serve, arrange the asparagus over four warmed plates. Pull the pork into tender shards and scatter over the asparagus. Break over pieces of crackling and add a little freshly chopped mint. Add a spritz of lemon juice and season with a little salt and pepper if required. Spoon over any resting juices from the pork before serving.

Pork and piccalilli sandwich

I get the impression that people don't know quite what to do with their leftover cold roast pork. On the whole, it's considered 'less versatile' than cold chicken or slices of Sunday's roast beef, and it seems there isn't a porky version of shepherd's pie. To me though, leftover cold roast pork is always good to have in the fridge. If it's been slow-roasted, then I make a simple version of rillettes by shredding the meat and combining it with a little pork lard and plenty of seasoning.

But, if I have some roast loin left over, then I like it served unadulterated but for a generous spoonful of piccalilli. This is not so much a recipe as a suggestion for the ultimate pork sarnie. You can make your own piccalilli (see below) or search out a good homemade version from a farm shop or local WI market.

Serves 1

A freshly baked roll or 2 good slices
   of bread
Unsalted butter, for spreading
2–3 thick slices of leftover roast pork
   (don't trim off the fat)

1–2 tbsp piccalilli
Sea salt and freshly ground
   black pepper

Split your roll and butter the bottom half generously. Lay your tender slices of pork on top, then spoon on the piccalilli. Season and devour with intent.

Piccalilli

Toss ½ small cauliflower, broken into florets, 1 cubed courgette, 2 cubed medium carrots, 1 chopped onion and 1 chopped small red pepper with 2 tbsp salt. Cover and leave to stand overnight. Put 2 tsp English mustard powder and 2 large pinches each of mustard seeds, turmeric, ground ginger, ground cumin, cayenne and ground black pepper in a pan with 250g granulated sugar and 500ml cider vinegar. Bring to a simmer, stirring until the sugar has dissolved. Rinse the veg in cold water to remove the excess salt, then drain well and add to the vinegar in the pan. Return to a simmer and cook, stirring occasionally, for 4–5 minutes. Mix 2 tbsp cornflour to a paste with 2 tbsp cold water, then stir into the piccalilli mixture. Bring back to the boil and simmer for 1–2 minutes to thicken. Spoon the hot piccalilli into sterilised jars and seal. It will keep in a cool, dark cupboard for several months.

My pork scratchings

I find the best way to make great pork scratchings is to create wicked crackling. I don't see the need to boil and blanch, or steam and fry: that's all such a fuss. I cut thick strips of dry skin with a healthy layer of fat on them and just whack them in a hot oven until puffed and crunchy.

Serves 4
300–400g pork skin from the shoulder
or loin with a 1cm layer of fat
Sea salt
Thyme leaves, to finish

Preheat the oven to 220°C/Gas mark 7.

It's essential that the pork skin is dry. If you keep it uncovered in the fridge overnight, this helps it lose moisture and it will 'crackle' more successfully.

Place the skin, fat side down, on a board. Take a super-sharp knife and cut the skin into 2cm thick strips. Set a rack over a roasting tray and lay the strips of skin on top, fat side down. Season with salt, then place in the hot oven for 20–25 minutes. Turn the oven down to 180°C/Gas mark 4 and cook for a further 15 minutes or until crisp and golden.

Remove the crackling from the oven and lift it off the tray. You will have a little rendered fat in the base of the tray. Pour this off and save it for your cooking.

Serve the pork scratchings warm, sprinkled with a little freshly crushed thyme and sea salt.

Pâté de campagne

This is a proper country pâté – beautifully moist, delicately textured and satisfyingly rustic. You need to either mince the liver and pork as described below or, as many pâté puritans suggest, chop it by hand. You can't blitz it in a food processor as the meat gets overworked and sticky. As it is a fairly delicate emulsification of liver, meat and fat, you need to be careful when cooking this pâté too. Overcooking, or subjecting it to too high a heat, will split the fat out and you might end up with a dry pâté sitting in a terrine full of fat and juices that should be held inside it.

Makes 2 terrines; each serves 8–10

500g very fresh pig's liver
500g fatty pork belly, cubed
500g fatty bacon trim, cubed
1 onion, peeled and chopped
2 garlic cloves, peeled and grated
A good pinch of ground mace
A good pinch of cayenne pepper
2 tbsp chopped sage
1 tbsp chopped thyme
75g fresh breadcrumbs
A wine glass of port
A wine glass of brandy
Sea salt and freshly ground black pepper

To line the terrines
18–20 rashers of rindless streaky
    bacon, soaked caul fat, or thin
    sheets of clean white back fat

Equipment
Mincer
2 x 1-litre terrines (or similar
    containers)
Cook's temperature probe

Cube the liver, trimming out any tough ventricles as you go. Place it in a large bowl with the pork belly, bacon trim, onion, garlic, mace, cayenne and the freshly chopped herbs. Mix thoroughly, cover and refrigerate for 2–3 hours or overnight.

Set up your mincer fitted with the coarse plate (7–8mm). Pass the meat and liver mixture through the mincer and back into the bowl. Add the breadcrumbs, port and brandy, season with some salt and pepper and mix well.

To achieve the correct texture, you need to pass the pâté through the mincer a second time. At this stage you can fry a little patty of the mixture, taste it and adjust the seasoning of the main mixture accordingly. Remember to compensate for the fact that this pâté will be served cold, which takes the edge off the seasoning.

Preheat the oven to 120°C/Gas mark ½. Line two 1-litre terrines with cling film, leaving some overhang around all the edges (wetting the inside of the terrine makes the cling film cling). Line the terrines with the bacon, caul or back fat as neatly as you can, leaving enough overhang to envelop the pork liver mixture within. Fold the overhanging bacon or fat over the pâté mixture, then do the same with the cling film. Cover the terrines with foil – or, if using traditional terrine dishes, use the heavy lids. Stand the terrines in a high-sided roasting tray and pour in enough hot water to come two-thirds of the way up the sides of the dishes.

Cook in the oven for 1½–2 hours. Check the core temperature of the pâté with a temperature probe; it should register no higher than 72°C. Alternatively, insert a small knife or skewer into the centre of each pâté, hold it there for a few moments, then remove and touch it to your wrist. If it feels very hot, your pâtés are cooked.

Remove the terrines from the oven and the tray of water and leave them to cool. Once cold, they can be pressed to achieve the correct texture. To do this, place the dishes on a tray, side by side. Find two pieces of wood that sit just inside the rim of the dish, covering the surface of the pâté. Sit another tray on top, weigh it down and refrigerate overnight. Don't be tempted to press the pâtés while they are still hot, as this will force out the lovely jelly, juice and fat you want to keep inside.

I think this wonderfully rich and well-flavoured pâté is best if left for a few days to mature. I serve it simply, with toast and chutney or perhaps a few pickled vegetables.

Pork pie

Sadly, petrol stations and corner shops haven't done this humble pie's reputation any good at all. Real pork pies are wonderful things and well worth the effort that goes into making them. I like to add a few prunes to my pork pie filling – they complement the meat beautifully, giving it a subtle sweetness.

Makes 2 pies; each serves 6

For the stock
A little oil
2 pig's trotters, ideally cut into pieces
    with a saw (or left whole)
1 onion, peeled and sliced
2 carrots, peeled and sliced
2 celery sticks, sliced
4 bay leaves, torn
1 tsp black peppercorns
1 tsp coriander seeds
A good pinch of salt
1 litre water

For the filling
1kg fatty pork shoulder or
    pork belly, cubed
500g homemade bacon, cubed,
    or good-quality lardons, or
    streaky bacon, chopped

6–8 pitted prunes, chopped
A small bunch of thyme,
    leaves only, chopped
50g fresh breadcrumbs
1 tsp ground white pepper
½ tsp ground black pepper
A good pinch of ground mace
Salt

For the hot water crust pastry
200g pork lard
175ml water
500g plain flour
½ tsp salt
1 egg, plus an extra egg for glazing

Equipment
2 x 10cm pork pie dishes

Start by making the stock, which will become the jelly that sits around the filling of your pork pie. Place a medium saucepan over a medium-low heat and add a dash of oil. When it is hot, add the trotters and cook gently for a few minutes. Now add the vegetables, bay leaves, peppercorns, coriander seeds and salt. Cook, stirring regularly, for 10 minutes.

Add the water and bring to a gentle simmer. Cook for 2 hours, topping up with fresh water as required.

Pass the stock through a fine sieve into a bowl, allow to cool and then chill in the fridge. You can save the skin and meat from the trotters for a crispy fried trotter salad, which is lovely with a poached egg.

To make the pie filling, mix the fresh pork with the bacon. Combine half this mixture with the prunes, then put it through a mincer on the fine plate (3–4mm). Chop the remaining meat by hand into 3–4mm dice. The best way to do this is on a big board with a large, sharp chef's knife. Alternatively, you can put all the meat through the mincer, but the filling won't have the traditional chunky texture that I prefer.

Re-combine all the chopped and minced meat in a bowl. Add the chopped thyme and breadcrumbs, and season well with the white and black pepper, mace and salt. Cover and refrigerate until needed.

Preheat the oven to 180°C/Gas mark 4.

To make the pastry, put the lard and water into a pan and warm them over a low heat until the fat has melted and the mixture is warm – it doesn't have to boil. Combine the flour with the salt in a large mixing bowl. Lightly beat the egg in another bowl. Pour the lard and water mixture into the flour. Add the beaten egg and bring together to form a dough. Gather the dough up and place on a work surface. Fold the pastry 4 or 5 times until smooth.

Divide the pastry in two, one for each pie. Take the first half and cut off a quarter; set this aside for the pie lid. Use the larger piece for the base and sides: form it into a round and then roll it out into a circle, roughly 15cm in diameter. Lay the pastry in one of the 10cm pie tins, carefully bringing it up the sides and smoothing out any pleats as you go. Leave a very slight overhang of pastry all round. Make sure there are no holes in the pastry or the jelly may leak out. Fill the lined tin with enough pork filling to come up to the top of the pastry.

Beat the egg for the glaze and brush the edges of the pastry with a little of it. Roll out the smaller portion of pastry for the lid. Carefully ease the lid into place and crimp the edges together in a tight, neat fashion. You may have to trim any overhanging edges at this point. Use the tip of a knife to make a small hole in the middle of the lid. Repeat this process for the second pie.

Bake the pies for 20 minutes, then lower the oven setting to 160°C/Gas mark 3. Brush the pies all over with beaten egg and return them to the oven for a further 1 hour, or until cooked through. Remove from the oven.

Warm the jellied stock until just liquid. Position a small funnel in the hole in the top of one pie and carefully pour in enough stock to come to the top. Repeat with the second pie. Allow to cool completely, then refrigerate overnight before eating.

Savoury Chelsea buns
with ham, spinach and hazelnuts

I shape and bake these in the same way I would classic Chelsea buns. Rich and crunchy, they're a perfect tear-and-share savoury snack. You can use kale, chard or even sea beet in place of spinach. Sea beet is a wonderful wild alternative to cultivated spinach and can be found growing in coastal areas. I use home-cured, tender smoked ham here, because I love the warmth it brings to the recipe, but a good-quality shop-bought ham will work equally well.

Makes 10 –12

For the dough
250ml whole milk, warmed to tepid
2 tsp active dried yeast
25g soft light brown sugar
400g strong white bread flour
100g rye flour
10g fine sea salt
100g butter, melted
1 egg, lightly beaten
A little butter or lard, for greasing

For the filling
About 250g spinach leaves, washed
1 tbsp olive oil
A knob of butter
1 onion, peeled and sliced
2 garlic cloves, peeled and thinly sliced
150–200g smoked ham, roughly chopped
100g hazelnuts, roughly broken
75g mature Cheddar, grated
2 tsp thyme leaves
Sea salt and freshly ground black pepper

For the dough, mix the warm milk, yeast and sugar together and whisk well. Leave for 15 minutes or so to froth up.

Combine the two flours and sea salt in a large bowl. Add the frothy yeast mixture, the melted butter and the beaten egg and mix to a rough dough. Turn out on to a floured surface and knead for around 10 minutes until smooth and giving. It's a slightly sticky dough, so you may want to flour your hands. That said, try not to add any more flour than you absolutely have to. You can do this in an electric mixer fitted with a dough hook but I find it more satisfying to use my hands.

Put the dough into a clean, lightly oiled bowl, cover with a damp tea towel or cling film and leave in a warm place until doubled in size. This may well take as long as 4 hours because the dough is so rich – and it certainly won't be risen sufficiently in less than an hour.

Meanwhile, for the filling, bring a large pan of water to the boil, add the spinach (or your greens of choice) and cook for 3–4 minutes or until the leaves are tender. Drain and, when cool enough to handle, squeeze out any excess liquid from the spinach and roughly chop it.

Heat the olive oil and butter in a large frying pan over a medium heat. Add the onion and cook, tossing occasionally, until it begins to soften and take on a little colour. Add the garlic, followed by the ham and cooked spinach, and cook for a further 2–3 minutes. Season well with salt and pepper, remove from the heat and allow to cool.

Grease a 35 x 25cm baking tray with butter. Carefully tip the risen dough out on to a well-floured surface and roll out to a rectangle, about 45 x 30cm, with one of the longer sides towards you. Brush the dough with a little melted butter or lard, leaving a 2–3cm margin at the longer edge furthest from you. Spoon the cooled ham and spinach mixture over the dough, spreading it as evenly as you can. Scatter over the hazelnut pieces. Season well with pepper and a good pinch of salt.

Now roll up the dough, starting at the long edge closest to you. Take your time as this can be tricky. Tidy up the ends of the roll by trimming them off with a sharp knife, then cut the roll into 12 equal pieces. Turn each piece on its side and arrange them in the greased tin so they all fit in. Scatter over the cheese and thyme. Carefully cover the tray with a damp tea towel, to stop the buns drying out as they rise. Leave them to rise in a warm place for 45 minutes–1 hour.

Preheat the oven to 200°C/Gas mark 6. Bake the buns for 20–25 minutes, until golden brown. Allow the buns to cool slightly before removing from the tin. Serve to friends with a full-flavoured bitter.

Big sausage rolls

I've always loved sausage rolls but it's hard to get good ones and even harder to know if the pork in them is free-range or organic. Far better to make your own...

Makes 8–10

1kg finely minced pork, ideally
    a mixture of shoulder and belly
A small bunch of chives, finely chopped
1 tsp chopped thyme leaves
1 tbsp chopped sage leaves
1 tsp garam masala
A small pinch of cayenne pepper
100g fresh white breadcrumbs
1 tsp salt
Freshly ground black pepper

For the rough puff pastry
175g unsalted butter, chilled and
    cut into small cubes
350g plain flour
A good pinch of salt
About 3–4 tbsp iced water, to mix
Egg wash (beaten egg mixed with
    a splash of milk), to glaze
Fennel seeds and flaky sea salt,
    to finish

For the filling, mix the pork with the herbs, spices, breadcrumbs, salt and pepper. Break off a little nugget and fry it so you can make a call on the seasoning. More herbs could be added or perhaps more cayenne if you like it hot.

To make the pastry, combine the butter cubes in a bowl with the flour and salt, then add just enough water to bring together into a fairly firm dough. On a well-floured surface, roll out the dough in one direction, away from you, to a rectangle about 1cm thick. Fold the two short ends into the middle so they overlap. Give the pastry a quarter-turn, and repeat the rolling and folding process five more times. Wrap the pastry in cling film, then rest it in the fridge for 30 minutes–1 hour.

Roll out the pastry on a floured surface to an oblong, about 45 x 12cm and 4mm thick. Lay the sausagemeat along one long side of the pastry, about 3cm in from the edge. Brush this pastry edge with a little egg wash and fold the other side of the pastry over the top of the filling to enclose it. Crimp the edges together well to seal.

Lightly brush the pastry with a little of the egg wash, then scatter over the fennel seeds and a light sprinkling of flaky salt. Place the sausage roll in the fridge for 10 minutes or so to firm up. Meanwhile, preheat the oven to 180°C/Gas mark 4.

Using a serrated knife, cut the sausage roll into 8 lengths and place on a baking tray lined with baking parchment. Bake in the oven for 35–45 minutes, until golden brown. Remove the sausage rolls from the tray to a wire rack to cool. Eat warm or leave to cool before serving. They can be kept in the fridge for a day or two.

Saucisson sec

Sometimes the simplest meals are the best: slices of saucisson, a little soft cheese, some good red wine and fresh bread, for instance. For me, this kind of food is pure pleasure – it is what it is, and it takes as long as it takes. There is no pretension in slow food like this. This air-dried sausage is made traditionally and allowed to mature over several weeks. Its rounded flavour and more-ish quality come from the gentle fermentation that takes place as it cures and dries.

Makes about 10 large saucissons secs

2.5kg lean pork from the shoulder
500g back fat, cut into 3–5mm dice
2 garlic cloves, peeled and grated
1 tbsp black peppercorns, lightly cracked
1 tbsp toasted fennel seeds, crushed
A glass of red wine

60g salt
6 metres beef runner casings, soaked overnight in cold water

Equipment
Mincer
Sausage stuffer

Pass the pork through the coarse plate of the mincer (7–8mm), catching the minced meat in a large mixing bowl. Add the fat, garlic, pepper, fennel, wine and salt. Mix well, cover and refrigerate overnight.

The following day, take your chilled mixture and load up the barrel of a sausage filler, fitted with the larger nozzle. Crank the handle so the mixture is forced to the tip of the nozzle: this will expel any air trapped inside.

Slide a length of beef runner on to the nozzle. Use a piece of butcher's string about 25cm long to tie the loose end of the casing with a tight granny knot. Make the knot in the centre of the length of string and about 3cm from the end of the casing. Flip this 3cm end over and secure it again, this time with a double granny knot. Fill the casing with the pork mixture to create a saucisson somewhere between 20 and 30cm long.

Use a second piece of string to tie off the end – a single granny knot will do. Then cut the casing 3cm above this point. You can then fold over this end and secure with a double granny knot.

Repeat this process until you have used up all the mixture.

Use a fine needle to prick any air pockets that you see in the saucissons, then put a loop in one set of strings so you can hang each one up.

Chorizo
24/7/04
$3 - 76?

Find a place to hang your saucissons. They want to be kept out of the rain and away from direct sunlight. A porch or lean-to is a good place – or maybe a small meat safe hung outside in the tree. I find we get really great results when we hang our saucissons in the stone shed in the walled garden at River Cottage. It has no glass in the south-facing window so there is a good flow of air – this really helps them dry. There is a door that keeps the cats out and it's cool on warmer days.

I hang the saucissons on nails that have been tapped into a roof joist. I don't let them touch each other as they age or they won't dry evenly. If the weather is dry, cold and windy, your saucissons can be ready to eat in just a few weeks, but when the weather is damp, dank and still, they don't dry as well. It's simply to do with the humidity in the air.

Check over the saucissons every few days. Look for that classic white bloom or mould typical of aged saucisson and salami. This is a good mould and one you should encourage. If you hang a shop-bought salami next to your saucissons as they dry, the bloom will spread.

I like to eat my saucissons secs when they still have a little give to them, and in normal conditions this could be after about 4 weeks. However, if you leave them hanging they will continue to dry, and the longer you leave them, the harder they will get. Use your thumb and forefinger to give them a squeeze, If your fingers leave an indent they might need a bit more hanging. When you're happy with them, take them down, wrap them in greaseproof paper and pop in the fridge. When ready to eat, peel off the membrane and slice into thin rounds.

If, for some reason, you have let your saucissons get overly hard you can use them to cook with instead of slicing them as you would a younger sausage.

Variation

Chorizo For a delicious, authentic air-dried chorizo, add 100g smoked paprika, 40g sweet paprika and a good pinch of cayenne pepper to the recipe above and then follow the same method for preparing and drying.

Home-cured streaky bacon

If you like cooking, then having a slab of your own bacon on hand is an absolute joy. Whether I'm braising big chunks of it with venison and orange, or frying thin rashers until crisp with scallops and sage, I find it brings amazing flavour. Making bacon is incredibly rewarding and easier than you might imagine. I don't use any artificial preservatives – just good-quality sea salt, a little sugar and a handful of aromatics to dry-cure the pork belly. Then I hang it somewhere cool to air-dry.

Makes about 2 kg

2.5kg piece of pork belly, ribs removed (see p.105)

For the dry cure
300g fine salt
200g soft brown sugar
2 tbsp lightly crushed coriander seeds
2 tbsp cracked black peppercorns

2 sprigs of rosemary, leaves stripped
A small bunch of thyme, leaves only, roughly chopped
2 garlic cloves, peeled and thinly sliced

Equipment
Shallow plastic food-grade box or tray

Combine the dry-cure ingredients, including the herbs and garlic, in a large bowl. Scatter a thin layer (about 50g) in the bottom of a clean shallow plastic box or tray. It needs to be big enough to take your piece of pork belly, but small enough to fit in the fridge. Lay the pork belly on the cure then scatter over another handful of cure (another 50g or so). Give the meat a quick massage all over, working in the cure, then pop it in the fridge. Keep the remaining dry cure in an airtight container.

The next day, pour off any liquid that's been drawn out of the meat. Apply a second layer of dry cure in the same way and return to the fridge. Repeat the process three more times (i.e. 5 days in total), using about 100g cure each day.

Rinse the cure from the bacon under cold running water then pat the bacon dry with a clean tea towel. Hang it up to dry outside (as for saucisson sec, p.221), out of direct sunlight, the rain and any animals partial to a little salted pork.

I like to air-dry my bacon for a couple of weeks before eating, to allow it to become firmer and develop flavour. Once the bacon is dry, you can keep it wrapped in a clean tea towel in the fridge for several months. If you make bacon regularly, you might like to invest in a slicer that enables you to cut thin, neat rashers. If you leave your bacon to hang for several months until it's firm to the touch, it can be eaten without cooking, like a good pancetta – try it thinly sliced with figs and honey.

Pressed pig's cheek terrine

This delicate, but wonderfully rich, terrine with its emerald marbling is a classic in the River Cottage kitchen. You'll need 4–6 pig's cheeks for this recipe, which seems like quite a few but actually, once they are cooked and trimmed, they don't go far. Pig's cheeks aren't expensive and a good butcher will happily order you up a batch. Lots of butchers just sell the trimmed 'cushion' of darker meat but you must ask for whole cheeks, as the fat and open-grained lighter meat is an important part of this dish. A couple of days ahead of cooking, the cheeks are immersed in a simple brine to lightly cure them.

Serves 8–10 as a starter

500g fine salt
2 litres water
4–6 pig's cheeks, depending on size
    (about 3kg)
2 onions, peeled and halved
2 large carrots, peeled
4 celery sticks, washed
4 bay leaves
3–4 sprigs of thyme
A large bunch of parsley, leaves only

1 tbsp capers
2 tsp mustard
2 tsp cider vinegar
2 tbsp olive oil
Scant ½ garlic clove, crushed
Sea salt and freshly ground
    black pepper

Equipment
A 1-litre terrine (or similar container)

To make the brine, combine the salt with the cold water, giving it a whisk to help it dissolve. Pour the salt solution into a big plastic tub and add the pig's cheeks. It's a good idea to weight them down so they all all submerged.

Leave the cheeks in the tub in the fridge or somewhere cool for 48 hours.

After the allotted time, take them out and dispense with the used brine. Rinse the cheeks under cold running water, then place them in a pan with the onions, carrots, celery, bay and thyme. Cover with fresh water and bring to a simmer. Cook, uncovered, over a low heat for 3–4 hours until tender. You may need to top up the water.

Meanwhile, on a board, chop the parsley leaves and capers together finely. Scrape this mixture into a bowl, add the mustard, vinegar, olive oil and garlic, season with salt and pepper and mix well.

Once the cheeks are cooked, carefully remove them from the pan and set aside on a tray or large plate to cool.

When the cheeks are cool enough to handle, peel away the skin and trim back any excess fat, but leave a good 1cm covering. Then remove the gland-type tissue from the underside of the cheek. You should be able to scrape this away, as well as any sinew or membrane, leaving the open-grained light meat underneath.

Line a 1-litre terrine with cling film, leaving some overhanging all round. I find if you make the inside of the dish slightly damp, the cling film will stick to it and the whole process is easier.

Spoon a small amount of the parsley mixture on to the base of the dish. Spread this out thinly. Now take some pieces of cheek and lay them evenly over the base of the dish as well. You may need to cut them to get a good fit. Make sure the grain of the meat follows the length of the dish, so when you slice the terrine you'll be cutting across the grain. Now, spoon over a little more of the parsley mixture followed by another layer of meat. Repeat until you have used up all the meat, or the terrine is full. Finish by spreading over any remaining parsley mixture.

Fold the cling film over the top of the mixture to enclose. Find something that will fit snugly within the edges of the terrine and that is practical to weight down. Place the terrine in the fridge with the weight on top and leave overnight to set. When ready to serve, take the terrine from the fridge and turn it out on to a clean board. Slice and serve with good bread or rye crackers.

A Christmas ham

I cure a ham each year. It makes lunch on Christmas day all the more satisfying and it's easy to do. You just have to think a couple of months ahead. I earmark a leg of pork from one of our late-autumn pigs, then towards the end of October, I'll think about getting it in the brine. I prefer to cure a whole leg of pork rather than a boned leg joint, as I like the traditional look of a baked gammon on the bone. That said, you can cure as much or as little as you'll need. A hock of pork will cure in exactly the same way, giving you a lovely ham hock after just a week or two.

Serves 10–12

**1 leg or half leg of pork,
   on or off the bone**

For the brine
2.2kg fine sea salt
5 litres water
2 litres good apple juice
2 litres cider
2kg soft brown sugar
A handful of black peppercorns

A handful of coriander seeds
1 tbsp cloves
2 bay leaves
A bunch of thyme
Pared zest of 2 oranges

Equipment
Large stockpot
Large plastic food-grade box

Put all the brine ingredients into a large stockpot, including the spices, herbs and orange zest. Bring to a simmer over a medium heat, stirring regularly to stop the salt and sugar catching on the bottom of the pan. Simmer for a minute or two, then remove from the heat and allow to cool. Pour the brine into a big, deep plastic food box, large enough to fit your pork leg in. Chill the brine until ready to use it.

You need to leave your pork in the brine for 3 days for every kilo it weighs. So if your leg of pork weighs 8kg, you'll leave it in the brine for 24 days. If you leave it in an extra day or two, it's not the end of the world. It might be a tiny bit saltier but you can rectify that by soaking the ham for a few hours before you cook it. When you're ready, immerse the pork in the brine, weighing it down so it is completely submerged. Leave somewhere nice and cool – it may not fit in your fridge.

After the allotted time, remove the ham and wash it under a cold running tap. Pat the ham dry with a clean tea towel and either hang it up in a cool, dry airy place or place on a tray in the fridge. I let my hams dry for 2–3 weeks before I cook them; they mature nicely over this time. However, a home-cured gammon like this can be cooked as soon as it comes out of the brine.

To cook your ham

Allow your ham to come up to room temperature, particularly if it's a big one on the bone and it's been in the fridge. It will cook far more evenly if it's not stone cold in the middle.

For the stock	For the spice bag
4 onions, peeled and halved	2 tsp cloves
4 celery sticks, washed and left whole	2 tsp coriander seeds
6 carrots	2 tsp mixed peppercorns
1 whole garlic bulb, halved horizontally	1 star anise
A small bunch of thyme	
A handful of parsley stalks (if available)	For the glaze
6 bay leaves	4 tbsp soft brown sugar
	About 4 tbsp English or Dijon mustard

Lower the cured ham into a pan large enough to hold it and cover with fresh water. Place on a medium heat and bring to the boil. Meanwhile, for the spice bag, tie the spices together in a piece of muslin.

Pour off and discard the water from the pan. Now add the stock vegetables, garlic, herbs and spice bag, cover with fresh water and place back on the heat. Return to the boil and cook at a low, low simmer, allowing 20 minutes per 500g. A large gammon, around 6kg, will therefore need about 4 hours' gentle cooking.

Once it is cooked, carefully remove the ham from the stock and allow it to cool slightly. Reserve the stock for soups, stews and risottos.

Meanwhile, prepare the glaze. Combine the sugar with enough mustard to give a thickish, spreadable paste and set aside. Preheat the oven to 160°C/Gas mark 3.

Use a knife to help you lift the skin from the ham: it should peel off quite easily. You can trim it back if you need to but leave a 1–2cm layer of fat all over the ham. Score the fat just down to the meat with the tip of a sharp knife in a crosshatch pattern. Place the skin in the base of a roasting tray that will hold the ham.

Place the ham on top of the skin in the roasting tray, then smother the ham with the mustard glaze. (You can, if you like, stud the ham at this point with lots of cloves, but I never bother!) Add a couple of ladlefuls of ham stock to the base of the tray (this, along with the skin, will help to stop the glaze burning), then place in the oven. Bake for 15–20 minutes per kg, but not for longer than 2 hours in total.

Allow to rest in a warm place for about 30 minutes before serving hot with parsley sauce, or leave to cool completely before serving.

Ham and pea broth
with lovage

Once you've cooked your ham, you'll be left with a beautiful, delicate stock – full of flavour and character. I freeze it in batches and whip it out when I'm cooking anything that calls for a good meaty stock. This soup, in all its wonderful simplicity, is clean, vibrant and refreshing. The unique, rounded flavour of lovage makes it particularly special.

Serves 4

1 litre well-flavoured ham stock
100–150g leftover tender ham
(see pp.229–30), roughly shredded
75–100g peas (fresh or frozen)

4–5 lovage leaves
Sea salt and freshly ground
black pepper

If the stock is cold, remove any fat that may have set on top of the stock, then pass the stock through a muslin-lined sieve into a clean pan. Bring the stock to a gentle simmer. Add the shredded ham and peas and cook for 2–3 minutes.

Finely chop the lovage and add to the soup. Taste and adjust the seasoning, adding pepper, and a little salt if needed. Serve with good, fresh bread and butter.

River Cottage prosciutto

In late autumn, we start curing our hams so they will be ready for the following year. They are packed in salt for about a month before being hung outside over the winter months to mature and gently dry in the wind. It's some of the best air-dried ham I've ever eaten and incredibly rewarding to make. This is real 'slow food', worth waiting for. I love to eat it sliced thinly, with good bread and fine olive oil.

Serves 2

1 leg of pork, aitch bone removed
  (see p.112)
1 sack of fine sea salt (about 25kg)
1–2 tbsp black peppercorns, cracked
  (optional)
1–2 tbsp coriander seeds, cracked
  (optional)
Malt vinegar

Equipment
Big scales
Large plastic food-grade box

I'd encourage you to cure your ham over the winter months when there are no flies around. Flies can spoil hams by laying eggs on them, so wait until late autumn.

Make sure your whole pork leg fits in your chosen plastic curing box. If it doesn't, place the leg on a board and remove the trotter (see p.113). You can either freeze or refrigerate this for another recipe.

Weigh the leg and give it a once-over, trimming away any obvious straggly areas of fat or meat; it should be nice and tidy.

Pour a layer of salt about 5cm thick over the base of the curing box. Lay the leg of pork in the box and rub it all over with a few handfuls of salt and the cracked peppercorns and coriander, if using. Turn the leg skin side up, then pour over enough salt to cover by at least 3cm, making sure the salt has filled all the nooks and crannies around the leg.

Find a board or tray that will fit neatly inside the curing box. Place this on top of the salted leg and place a heavy weight of 25kg or more on top of that. It's important to press the leg like this as it cures. You will need to salt the leg for 3 days for every kilo that it weighs. Keep the leg somewhere cool and dry during this time.

Once cured, remove the ham from the salt and wash it under a cold running tap. Rub it all over with malt vinegar, then hang it somewhere cool and airy to dry. A porch or lean-to where there is a good air circulation will work well. The ham will need to hang for 8–12 months before it's ready to slice and eat. The drying time depends enormously on the weather. A wet winter may slow things down, whereas a dry, windy winter will hurry the process along. During this time, your hams should have a nice dry surface with a healthy white bloom.

In the spring, the flies will return, and although your ham will be quite dry by then, it can pay to wrap it loosely in muslin until it's ready to eat. You can also get 'jambon sacks' – muslin bags specifically designed for ageing your hams outside.

A drying ham should feel dry and firm to the touch. It should look and smell tempting and carry a light powdery white bloom or mould. This is 'good mould' and will contribute towards the overall flavour of your ham. If your ham is sticky or covered in black, green or orange mould it should be treated with suspicion, as it may mean your ham isn't drying properly or hasn't been salted for long enough.

There's no right or wrong time to start eating your ham. As long as it's really firm to the touch, then it should be good to go. Some people like their hams young, while others like to mature them for years. It's a question of texture and flavours over time – and patience. At River Cottage, we start eating our air-dried hams at around 9 or 10 months.

To serve, trim back the hard outer skin, using a sharp knife, to reveal the tender, sweet, dark ham inside. Slice the ham thinly and enjoy with good bread and olive oil, and some ripe tomatoes.

Pork rillettes

This classic French preparation of seasoned, shredded pork belly, gently cooked in its own fat, is one of the finest preserved pork dishes I know. It's unrivalled spread thickly on toast with some cornichons and a glass of red wine.

Serves 10–12

1.5kg rindless pork belly
3–4 garlic cloves, bashed
A small bunch of thyme
6 bay leaves

500g rendered pork fat
    (from flare fat or back fat)
200ml water
Salt and freshly ground black pepper

Preheat the oven to 130°C/Gas mark ¾.

Cut the pork belly into thick pieces, 8–10cm long. Rub them all over with plenty of salt and pepper, then place in a large deep-sided roasting tray into which they fit in a single layer and fairly snugly. Tuck in the garlic cloves, thyme sprigs and bay leaves, then spoon on the fat and pour in the water. Cover the tray with foil, sealing the edges well. Place in the oven and cook for 3–4 hours, or until the meat is meltingly tender.

Classically the cooked pork for rillettes is shredded using two forks along its grain, resulting in tender strands. It's a technique that works really well. However, when I make a large batch, I sometimes use the end of a wooden rolling pin to lightly bash the pork, which is quicker, although puritans might frown at this approach.

Put all the finely shredded pork and fat into a large bowl, discarding any membrane, cartilage or bone.

Strain the cooking fat and stock through a fine sieve into a clean jug. You'll need about 500ml of liquor. Mix well, then ladle this liquor over the pork and combine well. Keep any remaining cooking liquor in the fridge and once it's cold you will be able to split the set fat from the stock and use them both for other recipes.

Season the rillettes with salt and pepper to taste then pack the mixture into sterilised jars (see p.243) or ramekins or just spoon into a bowl. Cover and chill in the fridge until set. Rillettes made like this will keep for up to 10 days in the fridge.

Smalec

Smalec is a traditional and totally wonderful Polish preparation for pork lard. Andrew Tyrell, a friend and talented chef, first made it for me and this is his recipe. You can use other herbs, but marjoram or oregano work best.

Makes 4 small (200–300g) jars

1kg white pork fat (flare fat, back fat or a mixture)

200g bacon (smoked is especially good), diced

2 large onions, peeled and finely diced

3 garlic cloves, peeled and sliced into fine slivers

A small bunch of marjoram or oregano, leaves only, chopped

Sea salt and freshly ground black pepper

Equipment

4 x 200ml jars (optional)

Either mince the fat or finely dice it by hand; dicing gives a little extra texture to the smalec.

Put the fat into a heavy-based saucepan and place over a low heat to start to melt it, stirring from time to time. The low heat is important (Andrew gets told off by his Polish mother-in-law for trying to rush this bit).

Once the fat is melting nicely, add the bacon, onions and garlic and continue cooking on the lowest possible heat until the bacon starts to go a little crisp, the onion is soft, and the smell is irresistible.

Season generously with salt and pepper and add the chopped marjoram or oregano. Pot into sterilised jars (see p.243), or a suitable serving crock or dish and allow to set, then place in the fridge. It will keep in jars in the fridge for a couple of weeks.

To serve, take a large slice of freshly baked bread, spread generously with smalec and season with flaky salt. Take the second slice with a proper dill pickle, have a shot or two of vodka and continue until satisfied.

Rillons

If you're captivated by the idea of jars of deeply savoury confit pork belly sitting on your larder shelf, ready to be served up whenever you choose, then you should try making rillons – the much-loved speciality of the French region of Touraine in the Loire valley. Pieces of lightly cured pork are cooked slowly with garlic and thyme until tender and giving. They are then either eaten warm, with greens, potatoes and mustard, or packed into large jars and preserved. If potted properly, rillons will keep for several months in a cool dark place.

Makes a 1-litre jar; serves 8–10

1.5kg pork belly, ribs removed
  (see p.105)
2 tbsp sea salt
2 tsp black peppercorns, crushed
8 bay leaves, shredded
300g rendered pork fat or lard
1 whole garlic bulb, halved
  horizontally

A small bunch of thyme
A small sprig of rosemary
A glass of red wine
A glass of water

Equipment
A 1-litre or 2 x 500ml preserving jar(s)
  (optional)

Cut the pork belly into thick strips and then cut each strip into 3 or 4 chunks. Place in a bowl. Combine the salt with the crushed peppercorns and shredded bay leaves and scatter over the pork. Refrigerate for 8–12 hours or overnight.

After the allotted time, wash the pork belly pieces in fresh water to remove the salt. Preheat the oven to 160°C/Gas mark 3. Heat a large heavy-based frying pan over a medium-high heat and add 1 tbsp of the pork fat. Fry the pork belly pieces all over for 5–10 minutes until golden and caramelised. You might have to do this in batches in order to avoid crowding the pan.

Transfer the pork to a roasting dish or large, shallow casserole. Add the garlic and nestle in the thyme and rosemary sprigs. Add the rendered pork fat, wine and water. Bring to a gentle simmer over a low heat, then cover tightly with foil or with a lid and place in the oven. Cook for 2–2½ hours or until the pork is very tender.

To serve the rillons hot, remove them from the cooking liquor and divide among warmed plates. Bring to the table with good mash and lemony greens.

To pot the rillons, first sterilise your preserving jar(s). If they have rubber seals, remove them. Heat the oven to 120°C/Gas mark ½. Put the jars on a clean oven tray and place them in the oven for 20–30 minutes. Remove with a clean tea towel.

Carefully lift the tender pieces of pork from the pan and pack them neatly into the cooling jars. Set a fine sieve over a pan. Skim off the fat from the tray or casserole with a ladle, into the sieve. Keep the meaty cooking juices separate – they will make an amazing gravy for another time.

Bring the strained, flavoursome pork fat to the simmer, then ladle it, very carefully, into the jars, making sure you cover the pork by 1–2cm. Seal the jars and allow them to cool before refrigerating or keeping somewhere cool and out of the light.

When you're ready to eat your preserved rillons, remove them from the jar and scrape off the excess fat.

Serve either warm (as above), heating the rillettes through in a hot oven, or cold with warm crusty bread and sharp pickled cucumbers or cornichons.

Chocolate truffles
with pig's blood and fennel

This recipe was inspired by my friend Robin Rea, a master of great pork cookery. It's not for the faint-hearted or for those with an aversion to the red stuff. That said, it's not unusual to use the blood of an animal to enrich a recipe; it's a technique dating back thousands of years and one that spans many cultures. The very nature of this ingredient exudes opulence and commands intrigue – basically everything a truffle should do.

Please give these wonderful fennel-spiked chocolates a go if you ever get the chance. You'll need very fresh blood and good-quality chocolate, and an occasion to show them off.

Makes about 24 truffles

100ml pig's blood
50ml double cream
1 heaped tbsp honey
A pinch of sea salt

1–2 tsp fennel seeds
250g dark chocolate, at least 70% cocoa solids, broken into pieces
Cocoa powder, to finish

Half-fill a medium saucepan with water and bring to a very gentle simmer. Put the blood, cream, honey, salt and fennel seeds into a heatproof bowl that will sit over the saucepan.

With the heat on its lowest setting, sit the bowl over the pan, making sure the base is not in contact with the water. The aim is to cook the blood and cream gently until the mixture thickens, just like a custard. It should register 72°C on a cook's thermometer. Now add the chocolate and allow it to melt very gently, or it may split; it should be smooth and glossy.

Pour the truffle mixture into an 18 x 10cm tray lined with cling film. Level off the surface with a palette knife and chill until firm.

To serve, turn out on to a clean board, peel away the cling film and cut into cubes, working quickly as you don't want them to melt in your hands. Dust the truffles with cocoa before bringing to the table.

Useful Things

Directory

Farms Not Factories
pigbusiness.co.uk
Non-profit organisation set up to
inspire people to make better food
choices that facilitate local, healthy
and fair farming systems for people,
animals and the planet.

The Soil Association
soilassociation.org
A charity campaigning for planet-
friendly organic food and farming that
can provide a wealth of information
for anyone interested in food, animals
and the environment.

British Pig Association
britishpigs.org.uk
The official breed society, it maintains
the herd books for many traditional
pig breeds.

The Accidental Smallholder
accidentalsmallholder.net
An excellent resource providing help,
support and advice for smallholders
and aspiring smallholders alike.

Supplies for Smallholders
suppliesforsmallholders.co.uk
Everything a smallholder could need.

The Organic Feed Company
organicfeed.co.uk
Provides a range of feeds made from
100% organic ingredients for a variety
of animals, including pigs.

Solway Recycling
solwayrecycling.co.uk
Robust, good-looking recycled plastic
pig arks, in a range of sizes and colours.

Animal Arks
animalarks.co.uk
Good selection of traditional arks,
as well as plastic ones.

Weschenfelder
weschenfelder.co.uk
Supplier of all things sausage-making
and butchery. Excellent range of kit.

AW Smiths
awsmith.co.uk
Well-established supplier of butcher's
sundries, as well as bigger kit.

Rusty Pig
rustypig.co.uk
Great home-reared pork – fresh and
cured. Available to eat in or take away.

Helen Browning's Organic
helenbrowningsorganic.co.uk
Fine organic pork, bacon and sausages.

Bellair Haye Pork
bellairhayepork.co.uk
Fine rare-breed and free-range pork.

Denhay Farms Ltd
denhay.co.uk
Producer of excellent dry-cured bacon,
ham and sausages, using pork from
outdoor-reared British herds.

Acknowledgements

I would like to say thank you to my wife Alice for being so gracious, beautiful and patient and, in the throws of adversity, calm – thank goodness for patchwork. And to my two biggest critics, my daughters Isla and Coco: sometimes the things you think you don't like now become the things you love when you're older.

Hugh, I simply would not be in the position I am in today were it not for you. You are a food hero, a true gentleman and a teacher.

To my friend Nikki Duffy, who I've worked with for almost ten years, thank you so much – you're the best. I think we make a pretty good team.

Thank you to Gavin Kingcome for all his pictures. I will always remember our early morning trip with the Oxford Sandy and Blacks. You created artworks.

Special thanks to Natalie Bellos and Xa Shaw Stewart at Bloomsbury, who have made things so simple and fun. It's been a pleasure to work with such lovely people. Thanks are also due to Antony Topping at Greene and Heaton.

Thanks to Janet Illsley and to Will Webb: you're like word and picture cooks – you took all the ingredients and made them into something delicious.

Thank you to all the chefs at Park Farm, including, but not limited to, the amazing Gelf Alderson, the incredible Andrew Tyrrell and the quite marvellous and much missed Chris Onions, as well as everyone else, especially Bob.

Thanks to Dan Powell for helping me with all of my pig-related questions.

Thanks to my friend and colleague Steve Lamb – it's always a pleasure; keep on keeping it real.

Thanks to Rob Love and the wonderful Lucy B, Sally Gale and all the other great people within the River Cottage family who have worked with me over the years.

Thanks to my mum for cooking so beautifully for me and to my dad for being someone I've always looked up to.

Index

Page numbers in *italic* refer to the illustrations

River Cottage Handbooks

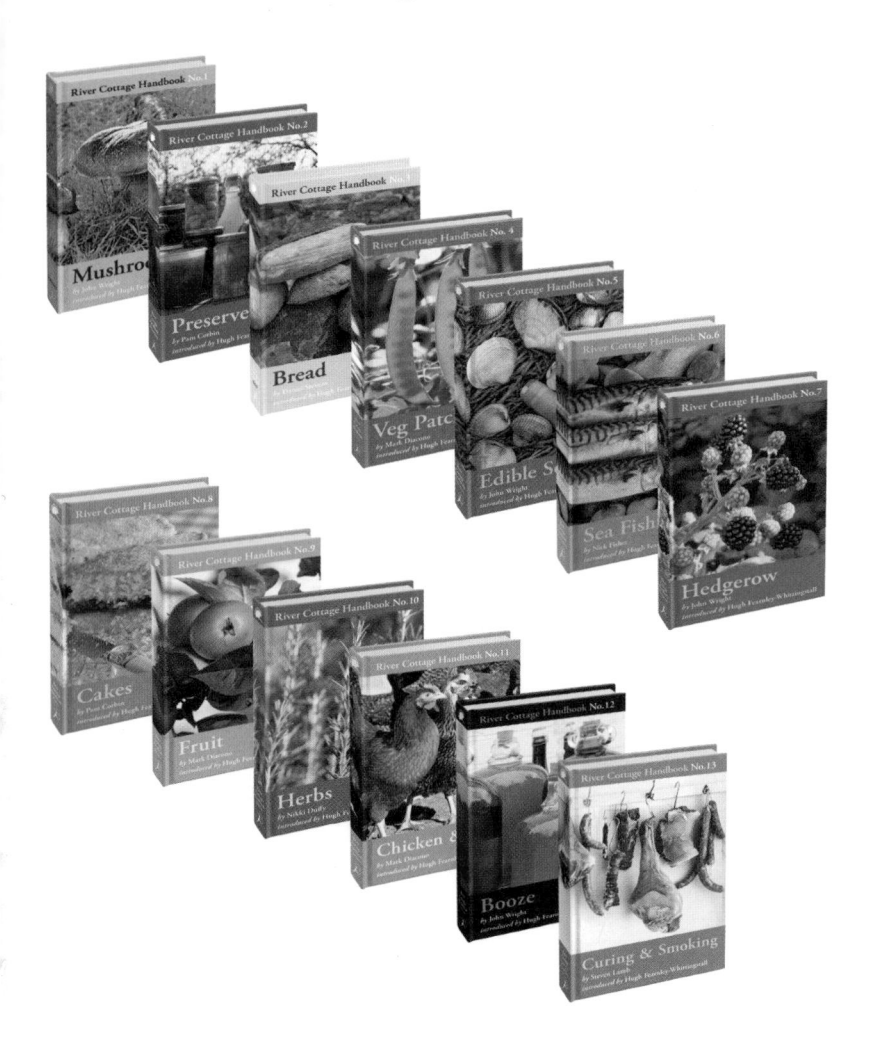

Seasonal, Local, Organic, Wild

FOR FURTHER INFORMATION AND
TO ORDER ONLINE, VISIT
RIVERCOTTAGE.NET